✝

I ACCEPTED JESUS CHRIST

AS MY LORD AND SAVIOR

On this _____ *of* _____ ,
                  (DAY)   (MONTH)

_____
            (YEAR)

Signed _____

My COMMITMENT

Have you come forward to personally accept Jesus Christ as your Lord and Savior?

☐ YES (Review pages 3 and 4.)

☐ IF NOT, which of the following statements best describes the action you are taking?

I HAVE ACCEPTED JESUS CHRIST PERSONALLY AS MY LORD AND SAVIOR BEFORE, BUT:

☐ I AM NOT SURE I HAVE ETERNAL LIFE, AND I NEED ASSURANCE. (Review pages 3 and 5.)

☐ I HAVE FAILED TO FOLLOW CHRIST AND WANT TO REDEDICATE MY LIFE TO HIM. (Review pages 3 and 6.)

☐ I WANT TO KNOW MORE ABOUT WHAT IT MEANS TO RECEIVE CHRIST. (Review pages 3 and 7.)

How to **RECEIVE CHRIST**

1. RECOGNIZE GOD'S PLAN—PEACE AND LIFE
The message you have just heard stressed that God loves you and wants you to experience His peace and life. The BIBLE says ... **"For God so loved the world, that he gave his only Son, that whoever believes in him should not perish but have eternal life." John 3:16**

2. REALIZE OUR PROBLEM—SEPARATION FROM GOD
People choose to disobey God and go their own way. This results in separation from God. The BIBLE says ... **"All have sinned and fall short of the glory of God." Romans 3:23 "The wages of sin is death, but the gift of God is eternal life in Christ Jesus our Lord." Romans 6:23, NKJV**

3. RESPOND TO GOD'S REMEDY—THE CROSS
God sent His Son to bridge the gap. Christ did this by paying the penalty for our sins when He died on the cross and rose from the grave. The BIBLE says ... **"But God shows his love for us in that while we were still sinners, Christ died for us." Romans 5:8**

4. RECEIVE CHRIST—AS LORD AND SAVIOR
You cross the bridge into God's family when you prayerfully ask Christ to come into your life. The BIBLE says ... **"But to all who did receive him, who believed in his name, he gave the right to become children of God." John 1:12**

HOW TO RECEIVE CHRIST
1. Admit your need (I am a sinner).
2. Be willing to turn from your sins, and ask God to forgive you (repent).
3. Believe that Jesus Christ died for you on the cross and rose from the grave.
4. Through prayer, invite Jesus Christ to come in and control your life through the Holy Spirit (receive Christ as Lord and Savior).

PRAYER OF COMMITMENT
Dear God, I know that I am a sinner. I want to turn from my sins, and I ask for Your forgiveness. I believe that Jesus Christ is Your Son. I believe He died for my sins and that You raised Him to life. I want Him to come into my heart and to take control of my life. I want to trust Jesus as my Savior and follow Him as my Lord from this day forward. In Jesus' Name, amen.

SALVATION *(First-time decision)*

When you prayed, committing your life to Christ, what happened?

Jesus said, **"Behold, I stand at the door and knock. If anyone hears my voice and opens the door, I will <u>come in</u> to him and eat with him, and he with me." Revelation 3:20**

1. What did Jesus say He would do if you asked Him into your life?

   "I will _____ ____."

   The BIBLE says ... **"But to all who did receive him, who believed in his name, he gave the right to become <u>children</u> of God." John 1:12**

2. What happened when you received Him?

   I became one of God's _____.

   The BIBLE says ... **"For God so loved the world, that he gave his only Son, that whoever believes in him should not perish but have <u>eternal life</u>." John 3:16**

3. Now that you believe in Jesus Christ and have asked Him to forgive your sins, what can you be certain of?

   I have _____ _____.

How do you know ...
you are saved?
you are a child of God?
you have eternal life?

I know because ...
God said it in His Word, and His truth will never change.

HOW TO BE SURE YOU HAVE ETERNAL LIFE *(Assurance)*

If you have committed your life to Christ, what does this guarantee?

The BIBLE says ... **"For God so loved the world that He gave His only begotten Son, that whoever believes in Him should not perish but have <u>everlasting life</u>." John 3:16, NKJV**

1. If you believe in Christ, what can you know with certainty?
   I have_____ _____.

Jesus says ... **"My sheep hear my voice, and I know them, and they follow me. I give them <u>eternal</u> <u>life</u>, and they will <u>never</u> <u>perish</u>, and no one will <u>snatch</u> them out of my <u>hand</u>. My Father, who has given them to me, is greater than all, and no one is able to <u>snatch</u> them out of the Father's <u>hand</u>." John 10:27-29**

2. What are you promised?
   - "I give them _____ _____."
   - "And they will _____ _____."
   - "No one will _____ them out of my _____."
   - "No one is able to _____ them out of the Father's _____."

How do you know ...
you are forgiven?
you are cleansed?
you are restored?

I know because ...
God said it in His Word, and His truth will never change.

HOW TO COME BACK TO CHRIST
(*Recommitment*)

If you have failed in following Christ and you are sorry and want to come back to Him, what must you do?

1. Confess your sins.

   The BIBLE says ... **"If we confess our sins, he is faithful and just to forgive us our sins and to cleanse us from all unrighteousness." 1 John 1:9**

- What must we do to be forgiven?
  _____ _____ _____.

- What does God say He will do if we confess?
  _____ ____.

  Confess means to agree with God. (e.g., I lied, I cheated, I was unkind, I lost my temper.)
- Right now, be specific with God ... Silently confess your sins to Him.

2. Surrender your life to God's control.

   The BIBLE says ... **"Do not present your members to sin ... but present yourselves to God." Romans 6:13**

- Walking with Christ means that we should offer ourselves to _____.

3. Ask for His strength daily to stay on God's pathway.

   The BIBLE says ... **"I can do all things through Christ who strengthens me." Philippians 4:13, NKJV**

- What can you do with God's help? _____ _____.
- What is it that God does in us? He _____ _____.

How do you know ...	I know because ...
you are forgiven? you are cleansed? you are restored?	God said it in His Word, and His truth will never change.

Know **MORE**

Jesus said, **"I am the way, the truth, and the life. No one comes to the Father except through Me."** **John 14:6, NKJV**

The BIBLE says ... **"These are written that you may believe that Jesus is the Christ, the Son of God, and that believing you may have life in His name."** **John 20:31, NKJV**

A Christian is someone who believes in Jesus Christ as Lord and Savior. Following are helpful steps to guide you:

1. Complete the studies in *Living in Christ* (beginning on page 14).
2. Begin to read the gospel of John, using the daily Bible reading guide on pages 50–51.
3. Pray daily, asking the Holy Spirit to guide you.
4. Ask others who are already Christians to help you.
5. Go to other groups and meetings arranged to help explain the Gospel, especially in the local church.

REMEMBER ...

You can receive Christ at any time by praying a prayer similar to the one on the bottom of page 3.

"Ask, and it will be given to you; seek, and you will find; knock, and it will be opened to you. For everyone who asks receives, and the one who seeks finds, and to the one who knocks it will be opened." **Matthew 7:7–8**

God said it in His Word, and His truth will never change.

LIVING IN CHRIST

& GOSPEL OF JOHN

A WORD OF ENCOURAGEMENT FROM FRANKLIN GRAHAM:

Congratulations on your decision to trust and follow Jesus Christ! You have taken an important step toward growing in a new and enduring relationship with Him.

Jesus said, "*I came that they may have life and have it abundantly*" (John 10:10). God wants you to experience full, eternal life, and He will help you. Here are some wonderful truths:

First, **the Bible is food for your spiritual life**. Just as your body needs daily nourishment, so does your walk with Christ. Through His Word, God will speak to you, strengthen you, and reveal His plan for you. I encourage you to read the gospel of John first. Then continue reading the Bible—try for a chapter a day. Before long, it will become a part of your daily practice and will change your life.

To help you understand more of God's Word, this book contains a four-lesson Bible study called *Living in Christ*, along with some Scripture verses you can memorize. This will help you grow in your walk with Christ, so I urge you to get started on these right away.

Second, **prayer is your lifeline to God**. Be sure to start each day with a few minutes in prayer. It may seem strange at first, and you may find it hard to know what to say, but God wants you to talk to Him as you would your dearest friend. The more you pray, the more natural it will become. Ask Him for His guidance and help. Then pray throughout the day as needs arise and, sometimes, just to tell Him thank you. Take your problems and burdens to God, because He is interested in everything you do. The Bible says, "[*Cast*] *all your anxieties on him, because he cares for you*" (1 Peter 5:7).

Third, **God wants to use you as a witness of His love and power with others in your life**. The Bible calls Christians "*ambassadors for Christ*" (2 Corinthians 5:20). This doesn't mean that you go up and down the street confronting everyone you meet. But start living a life that is different, then pray each day for the opportunity to share with someone else how He has changed your life. Even if you feel a little uncertain at first, trust Him to help you—He will. Before long, you could have the joy of introducing somebody else to Him.

Fourth, **God's design for us is to be in fellowship with other followers of Christ**. If you are not already involved in a local church, find one where the Word of God is faithfully proclaimed. He will bless you, and bless others through you, as you worship and serve Him together.

The step of faith you have taken does not mean that all your problems will automatically go away. In fact, you may have some new ones! The devil, who is God's enemy and yours, will try to spoil the work God is doing in you. He is a liar and will try to fill you with doubt and discouragement. But Jesus is the Truth, and relying on His Word is the way to defeat Satan. Follow the example of Jesus when He was tempted in the wilderness. Each time the devil tempted Him, He responded by quoting Scripture (see Matthew 4:4, 7, 10).

The following pages contain promises and assurances that will provide a good foundation for your life as a Christian, so read and reread them often. As you do, I'm confident you will experience the Lord's presence and help.

May God richly bless you,

Franklin Graham

HOW TO USE THIS BOOKLET

Living in Christ contains four Bible study lessons based on verses from the gospel of John and other books from the Bible. We encourag you to meet with another Christian as you study this section.

ASK

You may have received this booklet from someone who explained the Gospel to you. If you are at all unclear as to what this Gospel is all about, you should find Lessons 1 and 4 helpful. If you still have questions, ask a pastor or a trusted Christian friend to share his or her further insights with you.

READ

Read "A Word of Encouragement" on the preceding pages. In addition, begin reading the gospel of John. (Try the "Daily Bible Reading" plan on pages 50–51.)

STUDY

Read carefully the four lessons in this series, and answer the questions following each lesson:

1. **Knowing Christ** to help you begin your new life in Christ
2. **Growing in Christ** to show you the essentials to Christian growth
3. **Obeying Christ** to help you put first things first
4. **Witnessing for Christ** to help you win your friends to Christ

MEMORIZE

Detach the verse card (with a verse printed on each side) for each lesson as you study that lesson. Carry it with you. Memorize the two verses per lesson, beginning with John 3:16.

REFLECT

Think deeply about the Scriptures as you study and memorize. Talk about them with a Christian friend. Ask God to help you understand His Word and find specific and practical ways you can apply it to your life.

LESSON 1
KNOWING CHRIST

Whether you have just become a Christian or are renewing your commitment to Christ, let's review some basic truths about Jesus Christ and the salvation He offers. We can never really know enough about the Good News that has freed us from eternal death and given us eternal life!

OUR NEED FOR SALVATION

The Bible says, "*All have sinned and fall short of the glory of God*" (Romans 3:23). All people are sinners and are under God's judgment. The Bible shows this clearly, and common sense shows it as well. Though you may know many people who seem to be morally "better" than others, you probably don't know anyone who never makes a mistake.

The consequence of human sin and imperfection is eternal separation from God, who is holy and perfect. And since God is the very source of life, eternal separation from Him means eternal death: "*For the wages of sin is death*" (Romans 6:23).

PROMISE 1: THE PROMISE OF SALVATION

The Bible talks about something called "salvation," which means being set free from the consequences of sin (eternal death) and experiencing peace with God and the assurance that we can live forever with Him. John 3:16, perhaps the best-known verse in the Bible, explains clearly how you can have salvation and eternal life:

"*For God so loved the world, that he gave his only Son, that whoever believes in him should not perish but have eternal life.*"

John 3:16

Let's look at this verse one phrase at a time to better understand the simple truth it proclaims: "*For God so loved the world ...*"

The world includes you and every other individual on the face of the earth. God does love you, and the next part of the verse shows just how much He loves you: "*... that he gave his only Son ...*"

How did God give His Son? "*God shows his love for us in that while we were still sinners, Christ died for us*" (Romans 5:8). Jesus Christ, the Son of God, paid the penalty for your sins when He died on the cross. He took all your sins and died once for all. As He died He said, "*It is finished*" (John 19:30), meaning that He had truly done everything necessary for your salvation.

As the Son of God, Jesus is equal to God Himself. He is part of what theologians call the Trinity: God the Father, God the Son, and God the Holy Spirit. Amazingly, however, even though Jesus was equal to God the Father (John 1:1–3; 10:30), He freely chose to become a human being and die for us (Philippians 2:5–8).

How should you respond to Christ's death on the cross?

"*... that whoever believes in him should not perish ...*" If you believe that Jesus Christ is God's Son and accept Him as your Savior, you will not have to pay the eternal penalty for your sins—because Jesus paid that penalty for you when He died on the cross.

"*... but have eternal life.*" Instead of eternal death and separation from God, you will have eternal life. Eternal life is a present possession for all who believe. The moment you trust Christ,

- Your sins are forgiven (Colossians 1:14).
- You become a child of God (John 1:12).
- You possess eternal life (John 3:16).

Have you personally trusted Jesus Christ as your Lord and Savior? If so, then on the authority of God's Word you have eternal life. **If not, you can trust Him right now!** The Bible says,

"*Everyone who calls on the name of the Lord will be saved*" (Romans 10:13). You can receive Jesus Christ into your life right now by praying a prayer such as this:

Dear God,
I know that I am a sinner. I want to turn from my sins, and I ask
for Your forgiveness. I believe that Jesus Christ is Your Son. I
believe He died for my sins and that You raised Him to life. I
want Him to come into my heart and to take control of my life. I
want to trust Jesus as my Savior and follow Him as my Lord from
this day forward. In Jesus' Name, amen.

To be assured of salvation, simply take God at His Word:

"*For God so loved the world, that he gave his only Son, that whoever believes in him should not perish but have eternal life.*"
John 3:16

This verse is on one of the verse cards in the center of this booklet. Memorize it, and if you ever have occasion to doubt your salvation, use this verse as an anchor for your faith!

PROMISE 2: THE PROMISE OF VICTORY OVER TEMPTATION

If Satan cannot make you doubt your salvation, he will concentrate on some area of spiritual weakness in your life. Don't be surprised when this happens! Rather, learn to take your eyes off your own weaknesses and put your trust in Jesus Christ, who is able to help you:

"*I have been crucified with Christ. It is no longer I who live, but Christ who lives in me.*"
Galatians 2:20

When you are troubled by temptation, remember:

"*No temptation has overtaken you that is not common to man. God is faithful, and he will not let you be tempted beyond your ability, but with the temptation he will also provide the way of escape, that you may be able to endure it.*" 1 Corinthians 10:13

You may think that you are the only one who is tempted, but all believers go through similar tests. Temptation is not a sin. Even Christ was tempted (Hebrews 4:15). The sin comes only when you give in to the temptation.

To overcome temptation, take the problem to God immediately, before it has a chance to take root. Be positive in your prayers. Don't concentrate on the thing that is tempting you, but think about godly things:

"*Whatever is true, whatever is honorable, whatever is just, whatever is pure, whatever is lovely, whatever is commendable … think about these things.*" Philippians 4:8

Ask God to bring such experiences and thoughts into your life. Meditate on 1 Corinthians 10:13 (quoted above) and rely on its promises whenever you are tempted.

PROMISE 3: THE PROMISE OF FORGIVENESS

You will find that learning to live the Christian life is like learning to walk. There will be many ups and downs, especially in the beginning. This is natural, as the psalmist points out:

"*The steps of a man are established by the Lord, when he delights in his way; though he fall, he shall not be cast headlong, for the Lord upholds his hand.*" Psalm 37:23–24

The devil wants to trip you up and cause you to fall. Sin hinders our relationship with God, and Satan would love to keep you in a constant condition of being out of fellowship with God!

When you were learning to walk, you often fell down. But did you stay down long? No, you reached out to the extended hand of your mother or father, who put you back on your feet. This happened often, until finally you learned to walk. You can learn to walk with God the same way: When you fall, reach out to God through prayer, and accept His merciful helping hand:

"If we confess our sins, he is faithful and just to forgive us our sins and to cleanse us from all unrighteousness."   1 John 1:9

Whenever you do something that displeases the Lord, as soon as the Spirit of God has made you aware of it, make things right with God. As you do this again and again, you will come to know—firsthand!—the mercy and forgiveness of God and the joy of walking in constant fellowship with Him. Memorize 1 John 1:9 (on your first memory verse card) and practice it daily. Take God at His Word and believe Him for forgiveness and cleansing.

PROMISE 4: THE PROMISE OF HIS PRESENCE

Because you are human, it will be natural for you to doubt, to be frustrated at times, and to feel weak and all alone. But you are never alone; Christ is in you (Colossians 1:27), and He wants to help you become the kind of person He wants you to be:

"He who began a good work in you will bring it to completion at the day of Jesus Christ."   Philippians 1:6

He will meet your every need and will take care of you daily:

"*He who calls you is faithful; he will surely do it.*"

1 Thessalonians 5:24

"*I will never leave you nor forsake you.*"

Hebrews 13:5

You can also experience God's presence through His indwelling Holy Spirit. Jesus knew His followers' weaknesses and need for greater spiritual strength. He wanted them to know that even though He would not be present with them personally, the Holy Spirit, whom we have seen is a part of the Trinity, would take His place and meet their every need. He gave them this promise:

"*And I will ask the Father, and He will give you another Counselor to be with you forever.*"

John 14:16, HCSB

The Holy Spirit can be your Counselor or, as some Bible translations read, your "Comforter." He can also be your teacher. As you read your Bible and ask God to help you understand it, the indwelling Spirit will "*guide you into all the truth*" (John 16:13). He will also lead you (Romans 8:14), enrich your spiritual life (John 6:63; Romans 8:11), and empower you for Christian living (Galatians 5) and for dynamic witness to others about your faith (Acts 1:8).

The promises of salvation, of victory over temptation, of forgiveness, and of God's abiding presence are yours this very day. Practice God's presence, believe His promises, and walk in absolute dependence on His indwelling Holy Spirit.

LESSON 1
YOUR RESPONSE

Answer these questions by looking up the verses in the gospel of John:

1. What did Jesus come into the world to do? **John 1:29**

_____

2. How did Jesus take away the sins of the world? **John 19:16–18**

_____

3. God loved the world and gave His Son to die on the cross.
   John 3:16 tells how we can personally benefit from what God has done.
   (a) Fill in your first name in each of the following blank spaces:
      "For God so loved _____ , that He gave His only
      Son (Jesus), so that if _____ believes in Him,
      _____ will not perish (pay the penalty for sin), but
      _____ will have eternal life."
   (b) Physical life will end someday, but the life that God wants
      to give each one of us is eternal life, which means that it will
      never end. What must you do to have eternal life? **John 3:16**

_____

_____

4. What new relationship do you now enjoy by believing in
   Christ? **John 1:12**

_____

_____

5. What happens to those who do *not* believe in Christ?

   (a) **John 3:18** _____

   (b) **John 3:36** _____

6. Eternal life is not obtained by being religious, keeping a set of rules, or doing good works, but by believing in a person, Jesus Christ. What does Jesus say in **John 11:25–26**?

   _____

   _____

7. What happens the moment you believe in Christ?

   John 5:24 _____

8. Now review your answers and state briefly how you know that your sins are forgiven and that you have eternal life:

   _____

   _____

   _____

FINAL THOUGHT:

Now that you have received Jesus Christ as your personal Lord and Savior, claim the assurance of your salvation. As a child needs physical food each day to grow, a child of God needs daily spiritual food.

1. **Memorize the two verses for Lesson 1.**
2. **Go on to the next lesson, "Growing in Christ."**

NOTE: Suggested answers appear on page 43.

LESSON 2
GROWING IN CHRIST

God wants to meet with you—just you, personally—each and every day.

That thought may amaze you, but consider it for a moment: When you accept Jesus Christ as Lord and Savior, you become a member of God's family, a child of God. You can call God your Father. Any good parent wants to spend time with his or her children—sometimes with all of them together, but often with each one alone. That is how one person gets to know another person well—by spending time alone with that individual.

The best way to get to know your heavenly Father is to spend time alone with Him. You can do this by reading His Word and by talking with Him in prayer.

You can pray to God any time of the day—driving to work, preparing dinner, washing clothes, studying at school. But you also need to find a time during your day when you can give the Lord your full attention, without any distractions.

Perhaps the morning is best for you—when you are fresh, before your active day begins.

Or perhaps evening is best for you—at the close of the day, as you consider the next day's plans and prepare for a good night's rest.

Whatever the time of day, be consistent in your meeting with God. Jesus rose early to pray, and He went somewhere that was quiet—a good example for us to follow (Luke 5:16)!

There doesn't need to be any set order to your time alone with God, any more than there would be in spending time with an earthly parent.

A word of greeting should come first, a short prayer to God asking Him to bless the time. Then you will want to read some of His Word to you—the Bible.

If you are just getting acquainted with the Bible, you will likely find the gospel of John the most interesting, for it is here that God's plan of salvation is most beautifully summed up in one book. On pages 50–51, you will find a schedule for reading John in 30 days. After you have finished reading John, you may want to continue in the book of Acts to see how the early Christians shared their faith with those around them. Sharing your faith is one of the most important things you can do for God.

If you have not read much from the Bible, you may prefer to use a modern version. Ask your pastor or someone at your local Christian bookstore to recommend one.

While you are reading the Bible, meditate on what it says. To meditate simply means to think seriously about spiritual things. It means thinking quietly, soberly, and deeply about God—how wonderful He is, what wonderful things He has done for you, what He is going to do for you, and what He wants you to do for Him.

As you read the Bible and meditate, perhaps you will notice:

- a special promise to claim
- a guidepost for your day
- a command you should follow
- a searchlight pointing out a sin or spiritual need in your life
- a meaningful verse to memorize

Don't read too fast or try to finish too much at one time. Take time to look for all that God has for you in the day's passage. There's no need to rush through your time alone with God, especially if you spend time with Him each day.

When you have read and meditated awhile, talk with God in prayer. Talk to Him as you would to an earthly parent who loves you, who wants the best for you, and who wants to help you in every way possible.

Perhaps you do not know what to talk with God about. Perhaps these suggestions will help:

- You can **praise** Him for who He is—Creator and Sustainer of the entire universe, yet interested in each one of us!
- You can **thank** Him for all He has done, for all He is doing for you, and for all He has **promised** to do for you.
- You can **admit** to Him the things you have done or said or thought for which you are sorry. God tells us that He is both willing and able to forgive our sins (1 John 1:9).
- You can pray for your **family**. We have a special obligation to pray for those close to us.
- You can pray for **others**—for friends or neighbors who have needs, both physical and spiritual.
- You can pray for **yourself**. Ask God's guidance for the new day.

Ask Him to help you with any problem you might have. Ask Him to arrange opportunities for you to serve Him.

Try listing your prayer requests, so that you don't forget any and so you can record God's answers. (He may say "yes," or "no," or "wait.") Keep your list in a small notebook or on 3″ x 5″ cards—something small enough to fit in your pocket or billfold or purse.

If you have spent your time alone with God in the morning, continue your day refreshed and ready for whatever may come.

If you have spent your time alone with Him in the evening, go to sleep relaxed in His care, ready to rest for a new day of service to Him.

Better yet, try to spend some time alone with Him both morning and evening! (See Psalm 55:17.)

And remember that you can pray to the Lord any time, anywhere—in school, at work, at home—about anything—to ask for something you need or to thank Him for something you have received. As any loving earthly father would be, God is interested in all that happens to you.

He is looking forward to His time alone with you!

LESSON 2
YOUR RESPONSE

God speaks to us through the Bible, and we in turn can speak to Him through prayer. As we carry on this dialogue, we become better acquainted. This lesson should make Bible reading and prayer more meaningful.

1. Turn to the following passages in John's gospel, and briefly summarize the statements Jesus made about Himself.

   (a) **John 6:35**

   (b) **John 8:12**

   (c) **John 10:9**

   (d) **John 11:25–26**

2. What does Jesus promise if you keep His commandments?
   John 14:21

3. What further help is promised in **John 14:26**?

4. What does Jesus ask you to do in **John 13:34–35**, and why?

   (a) What does He ask you to do? **v. 34**

   (b) Why? **v. 35**

5. Read **John 21:1–6**. Describe what happened in verses 3 and 6.

(a) **v. 3** _____

(b) **v. 6** _____

(c) What important lesson can you learn from these verses?

_____

(d) What similar truth is taught in **John 15:5**?

_____

6. As a believer, what is now your privilege? **John 16:24**

_____

_____

7. As you grow in Christ, your faith and confidence will increase, and you will pray with greater assurance. What are you promised in **John 15:16**?

_____

_____

FINAL THOUGHT:

God the Holy Spirit is your teacher, and He uses the Scriptures to teach you. As you continue to read, study, and memorize the Scriptures—and pray—Christ will become more real and you will find fulfillment in life.

1. **Memorize the two verses for Lesson 2.**
2. **Please continue now to your next lesson.**

NOTE: Suggested answers appear on page 43.

LESSON 3
OBEYING CHRIST

As you grow as a new Christian, you will find it absolutely essential to make Christ your Lord as well as your Savior. You will never find true contentment and fulfillment until you have surrendered complete control of your life to Him. Perhaps the following questions will help you understand more about the joy of truly surrendering your life to God's control.

1. Study **1 Corinthians 6:19–20** and answer three important questions concerning Christ's lordship over your life:

   (a) Now that you are a Christian, what has your body become? **v. 19**

   (b) Why do you now belong to Christ? **vv. 19–20**

   (c) What should now be your purpose in life? **v. 20**

2. Briefly summarize what you think Jesus was teaching in the parable of the wise and foolish builders: **Luke 6:46–49**

   (a) What must we do if we call Jesus our Lord? **v. 46**

(b) What spiritual truth is represented by the house built on the rock? **vv. 47–48**

(c) What spiritual truth is represented by the house with no foundation? **v. 49**

3. What does the Apostle James say about obeying the Bible? **James 1:22–25**

4. Obedience to Jesus Christ as Lord is the true test of your commitment to Him. What does the Apostle John say about obedience? **1 John 2:3–6**

   v. 3

   v. 4

   v. 5

   v. 6

5. What is another sure way of knowing you belong to Christ? **1 John 3:14**

6. As you grow in Christ, there will be times when you fail Him. No one except Christ has ever lived a perfect life. Be willing to admit you have failed and confess your sin.

Briefly summarize what **1 John 1:8–10** teaches about confession and forgiveness:

v. 8 _____

v. 10 _____

v. 9 _____

7. What can you thank God for right now, concerning your need for God's forgiveness? **1 John 2:1–2** _____

_____

REMEMBER TO:

1. **Memorize the two verses for Lesson 3.**
2. **Please continue now to your final lesson. This could be the most important lesson of all. It concerns sharing your faith with others.**

NOTE: Suggested answers appear on pages 43–44.

LESSON 4
WITNESSING FOR CHRIST

As He began His ministry, Jesus called two fishermen, Simon Peter and his brother Andrew, and said, "*Follow me, and I will make you fishers of men*" (Matthew 4:19). Through the ages, the same call has gone out to all those who put their faith in Jesus Christ. He reaches the lost today through faithful witnesses like you. The Apostle Paul said that God has "*committed to us the word of reconciliation*" and that "*We are ambassadors for Christ*" (2 Corinthians 5:19–20, NKJV).

As you seek to be a witness for Christ, your life is a key part of your witness. Because you are a new creation, you need to demonstrate your new faith by your conduct. Jesus said, "*Let your light shine before others, so that they may see your good works and give glory to your Father who is in heaven*" (Matthew 5:16). This means your habits and lifestyle should commend the Lord Jesus Christ and help to draw others to Him. It does not mean that you must become perfect before you can witness. You surely will stumble from time to time as you are learning to walk. But as you learned in the last lesson, God is willing to forgive your sins and put you back on your feet again.

But living as a good example will not, in and of itself, make you an effective witness. You also need a power beyond yourself. That is the work of the Holy Spirit, who indwells all believers. The Bible says,

"*But you will receive power when the Holy Spirit has come upon you, and you will be my witnesses in Jerusalem and in all Judea and Samaria, and to the end of the earth.*"   Acts 1:8

When your life is clean and you walk under the control of the Holy Spirit, He is able to witness through you. For example, we read in Acts about a man named Philip who was chosen to serve the church because he was "*full of the Spirit and of wisdom*" (Acts 6:3). Philip was having a successful ministry in Samaria (Acts 8:4–13) when an angel summoned him to go to Gaza (Acts 8:26), where an Ethiopian official was returning from Jerusalem and reading from chapter 53 of Isaiah.

Using his God-given wisdom, and empowered by the Holy Spirit, Philip "*opened his mouth, and beginning with this Scripture he told him the good news about Jesus*" (Acts 8:35).

Your life is an essential part of your witness, and the Holy Spirit is indispensable in witnessing. But there is a third ingredient without which there can be no effective witness: the Word of God. In the witness of Philip, we saw how God had sovereignly placed the appropriate Scriptures in the hands of the Ethiopian. The Bible says that we have been "*born again … through the living and abiding word of God*" (1 Peter 1:23). When the seed, which is God's Word, is planted in a prepared heart, it produces the fruit of a new believer in Christ.

The question now is, **"How do I start witnessing for Christ? What do I say?"** To begin with, you can always share how Christ changed your own life. There is great power in a simple and honest personal testimony. It is also helpful, however, to have a practical outline in mind as to how you will present the facts of the Gospel.

THE GOSPEL MESSAGE

TRUTH 1:
GOD'S PLAN—PEACE AND LIFE

God created us not as robots, but as personal beings made in His own image (Genesis 1:27). He created us with the ability to relate to Him on an intelligent level. He gave us freedom of choice so that we could choose whether or not to love and obey Him. Just as we humans experience our deepest love from other humans, who have the freedom to accept or reject us, so also our Creator wanted a being who could love Him more than the rest of His creation.

When God had finished creating the world, He declared that everything in it—including human beings—was "*very good*" (Genesis 1:31).

TRUTH 2:
OUR PROBLEM—SEPARATION FROM GOD

Right away, God gave the humans He had created an opportunity to choose whether or not to obey Him. He placed Adam and Eve in a beautiful garden with just one regulation: They could eat of the fruit of every tree but one; to eat of that tree would mean spiritual death and separation from God (Genesis 2:16–17). Unfortunately, Adam and Eve chose to disobey God (Genesis 3:6) and were therefore separated from Him (Genesis 3:22–24). This separation exists today for all who are without Christ as Lord and Savior:

"*Therefore, just as sin came into the world through one man, and death through sin, and so death spread to all men because all sinned…*"   Romans 5:12

Even though Adam and Eve committed the "original" (first) sin, simple observation shows us that every human who has ever lived has been a sinner as well—as this verse states.

As a result of this universal sin, a chasm or gulf has become fixed between God and humans, as shown in the diagram below. Through the ages, people have tried to bridge this chasm in many different ways, but without success. As the illustration shows, they have tried various religions, good works, morality, and various philosophies of life to bridge the gap:

As we will see in step 3, there is only one remedy for this separation:

TRUTH 3:
GOD'S REMEDY—THE CROSS

Jesus Christ is the only answer to this problem of separation between human beings and God. When Jesus died on the cross and rose again from the grave, He paid the penalty for our sin and bridged the gap between us and God. His death and resurrection make a new life possible for all who believe in Him. The Bible says,

"For there is one God, and there is one mediator between God and men, the man Christ Jesus, who gave himself as a ransom for all."
1 Timothy 2:5–6

When Jesus Christ died on the cross, He made it possible for sinful people to be reconciled to God. The Apostle Peter said, "*For Christ also suffered once for sins, the righteous for the unrighteous, that he might bring us to God*" (1 Peter 3:18). Regardless of popular opinion that there are many ways to get to God, Jesus said,

"*I am the way, and the truth, and the life. No one comes to the Father except through me.*"   John 14:6

It is faith in Jesus Christ and not human effort that brings us to God. There is nothing we can do to earn our salvation. It is grace all the way:

"*For by grace you have been saved through faith. And this is not your own doing; it is the gift of God, not a result of works, so that no one may boast.*"   Ephesians 2:8–9

Yes, God has provided the only way, but we must make the choice. That brings us to step 4, the vital step of faith:

TRUTH 4:
OUR RESPONSE—RECEIVE CHRIST

We must all come to the place where we are willing to admit, "I am a sinner." Then we must be willing to repent, or turn, from our sins. The Bible says, "*Repent therefore, and turn back, that your sins may be blotted out*" (Acts 3:19). To repent means to change your thinking and to change the direction of your life. It means turning to Jesus Christ, who is the door to eternal life, the door to God and heaven. Jesus said,

"*I am the door. If anyone enters by me, he will be saved.*"
                    John 10:9

The door to forgiveness and salvation is through the cross of Christ. By faith, we must trust Him and receive Him as our Savior and Lord. When we do, we become children of God:

"But to all who did receive him, who believed in his name, he gave the right to become children of God." John 1:12

Eternal life then becomes a present possession:

"For God so loved the world, that he gave his only Son, that whoever believes in him should not perish but have eternal life." John 3:16

By faith we cross the bridge from death to eternal life through the cross.

Now let us look at the four steps as a whole:

God's Plan .... **Peace and Life**

Our Problem .... **Separation From God**

God's Remedy .... **The Cross**

Our Response .... **Receive Christ**

Which side are you on?

Here?................**or**................**Here?**

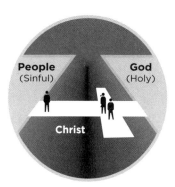

All you need to explain the Gospel using this graphic illustration is a pen and piece of paper. As you draw your illustration and explain the Gospel, try this four-step method of presentation:

STEP 1: EXPLAIN THE FACTS.

First, share the facts: On the top of your page, list the four truths presented on the previous page: "God's Plan," "Our Problem," "God's Remedy," "Our Response." List them one at a time and use a Scripture or two with each one.

After you list the first basic truth, "God's Plan—Peace and Life," read a Scripture or two and say, "Eternal life is not automatic, because we have a problem. Let me illustrate." Then draw the graphic of God on one side of the chasm and us on the other. As you draw, share the Scriptures that explain how the separation took place. Work your way on to the second diagram, showing how the cross bridges the chasm between us and God, and how we can cross the bridge through faith in Christ.

STEP 2: INVITE A RESPONSE.

If you feel led by the Spirit and the person is responding positively, proceed to the second step and offer an invitation, saying, "If this illustration is true—and I believe with all my heart that it is—then all of humankind is on either one side of the chasm or the other:

- "There are those who by personal faith in Jesus Christ have crossed the bridge and are now in God's family."
- "Then, there are multitudes who may be religious, striving to do good works and to be morally upright, but who have never committed their lives to Jesus Christ as Lord and Savior. They are still in their sins, separated from God."

Then ask, "Which side are you on? Here ... or here?" If the person is unsure or definitely realizes that he or she is on the wrong side, let the person know that he or she can be sure of his or her position by:

1. Admitting your need. (I am a sinner.)
2. Being willing to turn from your sin, and asking God to forgive you (repent).
3. Believing that Jesus Christ died for you on the cross and rose from the grave.
4. Through prayer, inviting Jesus Christ to come in and control your life through the Holy Spirit. (Receive Him as Lord and Savior.)

STEP 3: PRAY WITH THE PERSON RESPONDING.

The third step is the prayer of commitment. The Scripture says, "*Everyone who calls on the name of the Lord will be saved*" (Romans 10:13). Remember, Jesus Christ is the door to eternal life. Through prayer we can enter that door and receive Him as Lord and Savior. Lead the person in a simple prayer, such as:

Dear God,

I know that I am a sinner. I want to turn from my sins, and I ask for Your forgiveness. I believe that Jesus Christ is Your Son. I believe He died for my sins and that You raised Him to life. I want Him to come into my heart and to take control of my life. I want to trust Jesus as my Savior and follow Him as my Lord from this day forward. In Jesus' Name, amen.

STEP 4: CONFIRM THE NEW BELIEVER IN HIS OR HER DECISION.

If the person sincerely prays that prayer, he or she is a Christian and has been saved from eternal death! You will want to share some Scriptures to give the person assurance of his or her new standing before God:

What happens when we believe in Jesus Christ? The Bible says,

"*For God so loved the world, that he gave his only Son, that whoever believes in him should not perish but have eternal life.*"

John 3:16

And,

"*Whoever has the Son has life; whoever does not have the Son of God does not have life. I write these things to you who believe in the name of the Son of God, that you may know that you have eternal life.*" 1 John 5:12–13

Make sure the person knows that eternal life is a gift from our heavenly Father and that it is a present possession.

FOLLOW-UP

When you help a person in coming to faith in Christ, remember that this individual is a spiritual baby (1 Peter 2:2). In order to grow, an infant needs nurture and care. This means encouraging the person to immediately begin regular times of Bible study and prayer. You can do so by using this booklet:

- Share with the person the things you have learned from this booklet.
- This new Christian also needs the fellowship of other like-minded believers. Help him or her get established in a Bible-teaching church.

LESSON 4
YOUR RESPONSE

A witness in a courtroom tells what he or she knows about a given situation. The Christian witness tells others what he or she knows about Jesus Christ and what it means to personally trust Him.

1. What is the Good News (Gospel) that we should share?

    1 Corinthians 15:1–4

2. What power does the Gospel possess? **Romans 1:16**

3. What are three things an effective witness for Christ must have?

    (a) **Matthew 5:16**

    (b) **Acts 1:8**

    (c) **1 Peter 1:22–23**

4. Review the preceding message on witnessing and briefly explain the "Bridge to Life" illustration (pages 33–40).

5. Once a person is convinced of his or her sin and need of a Savior, what should that person do?

    (a) **Acts 3:19**

(b) **John 10:9** _____

(c) **John 1:12** _____

6. When a person believes in Jesus Christ, what can he or she now say with assurance? **John 3:16** _____

REMEMBER TO:

Memorize the two verses for Lesson 4.

NOTE: Suggested answers appear on page 44.

SUGGESTED ANSWERS

LESSON 1

1. To take away the world's sins.
2. He died, thus paying the penalty for our sins.
3. a. (Insert your name.)

   b. Believe in Jesus.
4. I am a child of God.
5. a. They are tried and condemned.

   b. They will not see life.
6. Believing in Jesus Christ means life forever.
7. I pass from death to life.
8. (Your answer.)

LESSON 2

1. a. He is the Bread of Life.

   b. He is the Light of the World.

   c. He is the Gate (or door).

   d. He is the Resurrection and the Life.
2. He will love me and show Himself to me.
3. The Holy Spirit will be my teacher.
4. a. Love one another.

   b. So others will know that I am His disciple.
5. a. The disciples went fishing and caught nothing.

   b. They obeyed Jesus and caught many fish.

   c. That I should always obey Him in all things.

   d. To have a fruitful life, I must abide in Him.
6. To pray to God in the Name of Jesus, which will help me find fullness of joy.
7. A fruitful life and answers to my prayers.

LESSON 3

1. a. A temple of the Holy Spirit.

   b. He bought me with His own blood.

   c. To honor God.

2. a. We should obey Him.

   b. We build strong lives when we obey Jesus and make Him
   our foundation.

   c. If Jesus is not our foundation, we lose everything.

3. We should hear God's Word and obediently act upon it.

4. **v. 3**: If we obey God, it shows that we know Him.

   v. 4: To disobey God while claiming to believe in Him
   is dishonest.

   v. 5: God's love is seen in the one who obeys Him.

   v. 6: We must faithfully follow Jesus.

5. If we truly believe in Christ, we will be filled with love for others.

6. **v. 8**: If we think we are sinless, we are deceived.

   v. 10: If we say we are sinless, it is the same as calling God a liar.

   v. 9: When we confess our sin, God forgives us.

7. That Jesus lives and intercedes for us.

LESSON 4

1. That Jesus died for our sins, was buried, and rose again, just as He had
   promised.

2. The power to save from sin all who believe.

3. a. A righteous life.

   b. Power from the Holy Spirit.

   c. A firsthand experience of God's love and forgiveness.

4. God loves us and has a plan for our lives. Because of sin, we are separated
   from God. God sent Jesus to be our bridge back to Him. To find our way back,
   we must receive Jesus as Savior and Lord.

5. a. Repent and turn to God.

   b. Receive salvation through Jesus.

   c. Receive Jesus and become God's child.

6. That he or she has eternal life.

HOW TO MEMORIZE SCRIPTURE

The four detachable memory verse cards on the next page are a very important part of your completion of this *Living in Christ* Bible study. After each of the four lessons in this booklet, you should memorize the two verses for that lesson. As you use each card, detach it and keep it in a convenient place for frequent review. Do you doubt your ability to memorize these Bible verses? Maybe these tips will help:

SAY IT ALOUD.

Say the verse aloud so that you can hear it as well as see it and think it. Do you ever find yourself thinking about a song you have recently heard? Or about something someone has said to you? The ear remembers! Use this built-in "memory chip" to help you memorize Scripture.

SAY IT THE SAME WAY EACH TIME.

Each of the four memory verse cards includes a topic name, such as "Applying God's Word," along with the verse and the reference. Each time you say the verse, do so in this order:

1. **The topic**
2. **The reference**
3. **The verse**
4. **Repeat the reference**

Reciting these four elements the same way each time will help you to firmly fix the passage in your mind.

SAY IT ONE PHRASE AT A TIME.

If you find the verse "too big for one bite," memorize it a phrase at a time, adding each phrase in order till you have the whole verse.

Even if you start with just three or four words, say the reference before and after the phrase.

SAY IT AGAIN AND AGAIN.

The real secret of Scripture memorization is review, review, review. Quote the verses often, asking God for deep understanding and seeking to apply each verse to your life.

Lesson 4

TELLING OTHERS ABOUT CHRIST

But you will receive power when the Holy Spirit has come upon you, and you will be my witnesses in Jerusalem and in all Judea and Samaria, and to the end of the earth.

ACTS 1:8

Lesson 2

CONFIDENCE IN PRAYER

And this is the confidence that we have toward him, that if we ask anything according to his will he hears us. And if we know that he hears us in whatever we ask, we know that we have the requests that we have asked of him.

1 JOHN 5:14–15

Lesson 3

CONFIRMATION OF MY LOVE FOR GOD

Whoever has my commandments and keeps them, he it is who loves me. And he who loves me will be loved by my Father, and I will love him and manifest myself to him.

JOHN 14:21

Lesson 1

PROMISE OF SALVATION

For God so loved the world, that he gave his only Son, that whoever believes in him should not perish but have eternal life.

JOHN 3:16

TELLING OTHERS ABOUT CHRIST

And he said to them, "Follow me, and I will make you fishers of men."

MATTHEW 4:19

Lesson 4

VICTORY THROUGH GOD'S WORD

How can a young man keep his way pure? By guarding it according to your word. ... I have stored up your word in my heart, that I might not sin against you.

PSALM 119:9, 11

Lesson 2

APPLYING GOD'S WORD

This Book of the Law shall not depart from your mouth, but you shall meditate on it day and night, so that you may be careful to do according to all that is written in it. For then you will make your way prosperous, and then you will have good success.

JOSHUA 1:8

Lesson 3

PROMISE OF FORGIVENESS

If we confess our sins, he is faithful and just to forgive us our sins and to cleanse us from all unrighteousness.

1 JOHN 1:9

Lesson 1

NOTES

NOTES

GOSPEL OF JOHN

& DAILY BIBLE READING PLAN

DAILY BIBLE READING

BEGIN TODAY TO READ PART OF JOHN'S GOSPEL, AND CHECK OFF EACH PORTION AS YOU READ IT.

❑ Day 1   John 1   Who Jesus Is

❑ Day 2   John 2   First Miracle & Cleansing of Temple

❑ Day 3   John 3   The New Birth—You Must Be Born Again

❑ Day 4   John 4   The Samaritan Woman

❑ Day 5   John 5   Jesus, the Son of God

❑ Day 6   John 6:1–29   Feeding the Five Thousand

❑ Day 7   John 6:30–71   Jesus, the Bread of Life

❑ Day 8   John 7   Jesus Teaching in the Temple

❑ Day 9   John 8   Jesus' Conflict With the Pharisees

❑ Day 10   John 9   Healing the Blind Man

❑ Day 11   John 10:1–21   Jesus, the Good Shepherd

❑ Day 12   John 10:22–42   Jesus Is Divine

❑ Day 13   John 11   Lazarus Raised From the Dead

❑ Day 14   John 12   Jesus Enters Jerusalem

"I am ᵃthe voice of one crying out in the wilderness, 'Make straight¹ the way of the Lord,' as the prophet Isaiah said."

²⁴(Now they had been sent from the Pharisees.) ²⁵They asked him, "Then why are you baptizing, if you are neither the Christ, nor Elijah, nor the Prophet?" ²⁶John answered them, "I baptize with water, but among you stands one you do not know, ²⁷even he who comes after me, the strap of whose sandal I am not worthy to untie." ²⁸These things took place in Bethany across the Jordan, where John was baptizing.

Behold, the Lamb of God

²⁹ The next day he saw Jesus coming toward him, and said, "Behold, the Lamb of God, who takes away the sin of the world! ³⁰This is he of whom I said, 'After me comes a man who ranks before me, because he was before me.' ³¹I myself did not know him, but for this purpose I came baptizing with water, that he might be revealed to Israel." ³²And John bore witness: "I saw the Spirit descend from heaven like a dove, and it remained on him. ³³I myself did not know him, but he who sent me to baptize with water said to me, 'He on whom you see the Spirit descend and remain, this is he who baptizes with the Holy Spirit.' ³⁴And I have seen and have borne witness that this is the Son² of God."

Jesus Calls the First Disciples

³⁵ The next day again John was standing with two of his disciples, ³⁶and he looked at Jesus as he walked by and said, "Behold, the Lamb of God!" ³⁷The two disciples heard him say this, and they followed Jesus. ³⁸Jesus turned and saw them following and said to them, "What are you seeking?" And they said to him, "Rabbi" (which means Teacher), "where are you staying?" ³⁹He said to them, "Come and you will see." So they came and saw where he was staying, and they stayed with him that day, for it was about the tenth hour.³ ⁴⁰One of the two who heard John speak and followed Jesus⁴ was Andrew, Simon Peter's brother. ⁴¹He first found his own brother Simon and said to him, "We have found the Messiah" (which means Christ). ⁴²He brought him to Jesus. Jesus looked at him and said, "You are Simon the son of John. You shall be called Cephas" (which means Peter⁵).

Jesus Calls Philip and Nathanael

⁴³ The next day Jesus decided to go to Galilee. He found Philip and said to him, "Follow me." ⁴⁴Now Philip was from Bethsaida, the city of

¹Or crying out, 'In the wilderness make straight ²Some manuscripts the Chosen One ³That is, about 4 p.m. ⁴Greek him ⁵Cephas and Peter are from the word for rock in Aramaic and Greek, respectively ᵃIsa. 40:3

Andrew and Peter. ⁴⁵Philip found Nathanael and said to him, "We have found him of whom Moses in the Law and also the prophets wrote, Jesus of Nazareth, the son of Joseph." ⁴⁶Nathanael said to him, "Can anything good come out of Nazareth?" Philip said to him, "Come and see." ⁴⁷Jesus saw Nathanael coming toward him and said of him, "Behold, an Israelite indeed, in whom there is no deceit!" ⁴⁸Nathanael said to him, "How do you know me?" Jesus answered him, "Before Philip called you, when you were under the fig tree, I saw you." ⁴⁹Nathanael answered him, "Rabbi, you are the Son of God! You are the King of Israel!" ⁵⁰Jesus answered him, "Because I said to you, 'I saw you under the fig tree,' do you believe? You will see greater things than these." ⁵¹And he said to him, "Truly, truly, I say to you,[1] you will see heaven opened, and the angels of God ascending and descending on the Son of Man."

DAY 2

The Wedding at Cana

2 On the third day there was a wedding at Cana in Galilee, and the mother of Jesus was there. ²Jesus also was invited to the wedding with his disciples. ³When the wine ran out, the mother of Jesus said to him, "They have no wine." ⁴And Jesus said to her, "Woman, what does this have to do with me? My hour has not yet come." ⁵His mother said to the servants, "Do whatever he tells you."

⁶Now there were six stone water jars there for the Jewish rites of purification, each holding twenty or thirty gallons.[2] ⁷Jesus said to the servants, "Fill the jars with water." And they filled them up to the brim. ⁸And he said to them, "Now draw some out and take it to the master of the feast." So they took it. ⁹When the master of the feast tasted the water now become wine, and did not know where it came from (though the servants who had drawn the water knew), the master of the feast called the bridegroom ¹⁰and said to him, "Everyone serves the good wine first, and when people have drunk freely, then the poor wine. But you have kept the good wine until now." ¹¹This, the first of his signs, Jesus did at Cana in Galilee, and manifested his glory. And his disciples believed in him.

¹²After this he went down to Capernaum, with his mother and his brothers[3] and his disciples, and they stayed there for a few days.

---

[1]The Greek for *you* is plural; twice in this verse [2]Greek *two or three measures (metrētas);* a *metrētēs* was about 10 gallons or 35 liters [3]Or *brothers and sisters.* In New Testament usage, depending on the context, the plural Greek word *adelphoi* (translated "brothers") may refer either to *brothers* or to *brothers and sisters*

Jesus Cleanses the Temple

[13] The Passover of the Jews was at hand, and Jesus went up to Jerusalem. [14]In the temple he found those who were selling oxen and sheep and pigeons, and the money-changers sitting there. [15]And making a whip of cords, he drove them all out of the temple, with the sheep and oxen. And he poured out the coins of the money-changers and overturned their tables. [16]And he told those who sold the pigeons, "Take these things away; do not make my Father's house a house of trade." [17]His disciples remembered that it was written, [a]"Zeal for your house will consume me."

[18]So the Jews said to him, "What sign do you show us for doing these things?" [19]Jesus answered them, "Destroy this temple, and in three days I will raise it up." [20]The Jews then said, "It has taken forty-six years to build this temple,[1] and will you raise it up in three days?" [21]But he was speaking about the temple of his body. [22]When therefore he was raised from the dead, his disciples remembered that he had said this, and they believed the Scripture and the word that Jesus had spoken.

Jesus Knows What Is in Man

[23]Now when he was in Jerusalem at the Passover Feast, many believed in his name when they saw the signs that he was doing. [24]But Jesus on his part did not entrust himself to them, because he knew all people [25]and needed no one to bear witness about man, for he himself knew what was in man.

DAY 3

You Must Be Born Again

3 Now there was a man of the Pharisees named Nicodemus, a ruler of the Jews. [2]This man came to Jesus[2] by night and said to him, "Rabbi, we know that you are a teacher come from God, for no one can do these signs that you do unless God is with him." [3]Jesus answered him, "Truly, truly, I say to you, unless one is born again[3] he cannot see the kingdom of God." [4]Nicodemus said to him, "How can a man be born when he is old? Can he enter a second time into his mother's womb and be born?" [5]Jesus answered, "Truly, truly, I say to you, unless one is born of water and the Spirit, he cannot enter the kingdom of God. [6]That which is born of the flesh is flesh, and that which is born of the Spirit is spirit.[4] [7]Do not marvel that I said to you, 'You[5] must be born again.' [8]The wind[6] blows where it wishes, and you hear its sound, but you do not know where it comes from or where it goes. So it is with everyone who is born of the Spirit."

[1]Or *This temple was built forty-six years ago* [2]Greek *him* [3]Or *from above*; the Greek is purposely ambiguous and can mean both *again* and *from above*; also verse 7 [4]The same Greek word means both *wind* and *spirit* [5]The Greek for *you* is plural here [6]The same Greek word means both *wind* and *spirit* [a]Ps. 69:9

⁹Nicodemus said to him, "How can these things be?" ¹⁰Jesus answered him, "Are you the teacher of Israel and yet you do not understand these things? ¹¹Truly, truly, I say to you, we speak of what we know, and bear witness to what we have seen, but you¹ do not receive our testimony. ¹²If I have told you earthly things and you do not believe, how can you believe if I tell you heavenly things? ¹³No one has ascended into heaven except he who descended from heaven, the Son of Man.² ¹⁴And as Moses lifted up the serpent in the wilderness, so must the Son of Man be lifted up, ¹⁵that whoever believes in him may have eternal life.³

For God So Loved the World

¹⁶"For God so loved the world,⁴ that he gave his only Son, that whoever believes in him should not perish but have eternal life. ¹⁷For God did not send his Son into the world to condemn the world, but in order that the world might be saved through him. ¹⁸Whoever believes in him is not condemned, but whoever does not believe is condemned already, because he has not believed in the name of the only Son of God. ¹⁹And this is the judgment: the light has come into the world, and people loved the darkness rather than the light because their works were evil. ²⁰For everyone who does wicked things hates the light and does not come to the light, lest his works should be exposed. ²¹But whoever does what is true comes to the light, so that it may be clearly seen that his works have been carried out in God."

John the Baptist Exalts Christ

²²After this Jesus and his disciples went into the Judean countryside, and he remained there with them and was baptizing. ²³John also was baptizing at Aenon near Salim, because water was plentiful there, and people were coming and being baptized ²⁴(for John had not yet been put in prison).

²⁵Now a discussion arose between some of John's disciples and a Jew over purification. ²⁶And they came to John and said to him, "Rabbi, he who was with you across the Jordan, to whom you bore witness—look, he is baptizing, and all are going to him." ²⁷John answered, "A person cannot receive even one thing unless it is given him from heaven. ²⁸You yourselves bear me witness, that I said, 'I am not the Christ, but I have been sent before him.' ²⁹The one who has the bride is the bridegroom. The friend of the bridegroom, who stands and hears him, rejoices greatly at the bridegroom's voice. Therefore this joy of mine is now complete. ³⁰He must increase, but I must decrease."⁵

³¹He who comes from above is above all. He who is of the earth belongs to

---

¹The Greek for *you* is plural here; also four times in verse 12 ²Some manuscripts add *who is in heaven* ³Some interpreters hold that the quotation ends at verse 15 ⁴Or *For this is how God loved the world* ⁵Some interpreters hold that the quotation continues through verse 36

the earth and speaks in an earthly way. He who comes from heaven is above all. [32]He bears witness to what he has seen and heard, yet no one receives his testimony. [33]Whoever receives his testimony sets his seal to this, that God is true. [34]For he whom God has sent utters the words of God, for he gives the Spirit without measure. [35]The Father loves the Son and has given all things into his hand. [36]Whoever believes in the Son has eternal life; whoever does not obey the Son shall not see life, but the wrath of God remains on him.

DAY 4

Jesus and the Woman of Samaria

4 Now when Jesus learned that the Pharisees had heard that Jesus was making and baptizing more disciples than John [2](although Jesus himself did not baptize, but only his disciples), [3]he left Judea and departed again for Galilee. [4]And he had to pass through Samaria. [5]So he came to a town of Samaria called Sychar, near the field that Jacob had given to his son Joseph. [6]Jacob's well was there; so Jesus, wearied as he was from his journey, was sitting beside the well. It was about the sixth hour.[1]

[7]A woman from Samaria came to draw water. Jesus said to her, "Give me a drink." [8](For his disciples had gone away into the city to buy food.) [9]The Samaritan woman said to him, "How is it that you, a Jew, ask for a drink from me, a woman of Samaria?" (For Jews have no dealings with Samaritans.) [10]Jesus answered her, "If you knew the gift of God, and who it is that is saying to you, 'Give me a drink,' you would have asked him, and he would have given you living water." [11]The woman said to him, "Sir, you have nothing to draw water with, and the well is deep. Where do you get that living water? [12]Are you greater than our father Jacob? He gave us the well and drank from it himself, as did his sons and his livestock." [13]Jesus said to her, "Everyone who drinks of this water will be thirsty again, [14]but whoever drinks of the water that I will give him will never be thirsty again.[2] The water that I will give him will become in him a spring of water welling up to eternal life." [15]The woman said to him, "Sir, give me this water, so that I will not be thirsty or have to come here to draw water."

[16]Jesus said to her, "Go, call your husband, and come here." [17]The woman answered him, "I have no husband." Jesus said to her, "You are right in saying, 'I have no husband'; [18]for you have had five husbands, and the one you now have is not your husband. What you have said is true." [19]The woman said to him, "Sir, I perceive that you are a prophet. [20]Our fathers worshiped on this mountain, but you say that in Jerusalem is the place where people

[1]That is, about noon [2]Greek *forever*

ought to worship." ²¹Jesus said to her, "Woman, believe me, the hour is coming when neither on this mountain nor in Jerusalem will you worship the Father. ²²You worship what you do not know; we worship what we know, for salvation is from the Jews. ²³But the hour is coming, and is now here, when the true worshipers will worship the Father in spirit and truth, for the Father is seeking such people to worship him. ²⁴God is spirit, and those who worship him must worship in spirit and truth." ²⁵The woman said to him, "I know that Messiah is coming (he who is called Christ). When he comes, he will tell us all things." ²⁶Jesus said to her, "I who speak to you am he."

²⁷Just then his disciples came back. They marveled that he was talking with a woman, but no one said, "What do you seek?" or, "Why are you talking with her?" ²⁸So the woman left her water jar and went away into town and said to the people, ²⁹"Come, see a man who told me all that I ever did. Can this be the Christ?" ³⁰They went out of the town and were coming to him.

³¹Meanwhile the disciples were urging him, saying, "Rabbi, eat." ³²But he said to them, "I have food to eat that you do not know about." ³³So the disciples said to one another, "Has anyone brought him something to eat?" ³⁴Jesus said to them, "My food is to do the will of him who sent me and to accomplish his work. ³⁵Do you not say, 'There are yet four months, then comes the harvest'? Look, I tell you, lift up your eyes, and see that the fields are white for harvest. ³⁶Already the one who reaps is receiving wages and gathering fruit for eternal life, so that sower and reaper may rejoice together. ³⁷For here the saying holds true, 'One sows and another reaps.' ³⁸I sent you to reap that for which you did not labor. Others have labored, and you have entered into their labor."

³⁹Many Samaritans from that town believed in him because of the woman's testimony, "He told me all that I ever did." ⁴⁰So when the Samaritans came to him, they asked him to stay with them, and he stayed there two days. ⁴¹And many more believed because of his word. ⁴²They said to the woman, "It is no longer because of what you said that we believe, for we have heard for ourselves, and we know that this is indeed the Savior of the world."

⁴³After the two days he departed for Galilee. ⁴⁴(For Jesus himself had testified that a prophet has no honor in his own hometown.) ⁴⁵So when he came to Galilee, the Galileans welcomed him, having seen all that he had done in Jerusalem at the feast. For they too had gone to the feast.

Jesus Heals an Official's Son

⁴⁶So he came again to Cana in Galilee, where he had made the water wine. And at Capernaum there was an official whose son was ill. ⁴⁷When

this man heard that Jesus had come from Judea to Galilee, he went to him and asked him to come down and heal his son, for he was at the point of death. ⁴⁸So Jesus said to him, "Unless you[1] see signs and wonders you will not believe." ⁴⁹The official said to him, "Sir, come down before my child dies." ⁵⁰Jesus said to him, "Go; your son will live." The man believed the word that Jesus spoke to him and went on his way. ⁵¹As he was going down, his servants[2] met him and told him that his son was recovering. ⁵²So he asked them the hour when he began to get better, and they said to him, "Yesterday at the seventh hour[3] the fever left him." ⁵³The father knew that was the hour when Jesus had said to him, "Your son will live." And he himself believed, and all his household. ⁵⁴This was now the second sign that Jesus did when he had come from Judea to Galilee.

DAY 5

The Healing at the Pool on the Sabbath

5 After this there was a feast of the Jews, and Jesus went up to Jerusalem. ²Now there is in Jerusalem by the Sheep Gate a pool, in Aramaic[4] called Bethesda,[5] which has five roofed colonnades. ³In these lay a multitude of invalids—blind, lame, and paralyzed.[6] ⁵One man was there who had been an invalid for thirty-eight years. ⁶When Jesus saw him lying there and knew that he had already been there a long time, he said to him, "Do you want to be healed?" ⁷The sick man answered him, "Sir, I have no one to put me into the pool when the water is stirred up, and while I am going another steps down before me." ⁸Jesus said to him, "Get up, take up your bed, and walk." ⁹And at once the man was healed, and he took up his bed and walked.

Now that day was the Sabbath. ¹⁰So the Jews[7] said to the man who had been healed, "It is the Sabbath, and it is not lawful for you to take up your bed." ¹¹But he answered them, "The man who healed me, that man said to me, 'Take up your bed, and walk.'" ¹²They asked him, "Who is the man who said to you, 'Take up your bed and walk'?" ¹³Now the man who had been healed did not know who it was, for Jesus had withdrawn, as there was a crowd in the place. ¹⁴Afterward Jesus found him in the temple and said to him, "See, you are well! Sin no more, that nothing worse may happen to you." ¹⁵The man went away and told the Jews that it was Jesus who had healed him. ¹⁶And this was why the Jews were persecuting Jesus, because he was doing these things on the

---

[1]The Greek for you is plural; twice in this verse [2]Or bondservants [3]That is, at 1 p.m. [4]Or Hebrew [5]Some manuscripts Bethsaida [6]Some manuscripts insert, wholly or in part, waiting for the moving of the water; ⁴for an angel of the Lord went down at certain seasons into the pool, and stirred the water: whoever stepped in first after the stirring of the water was healed of whatever disease he had [7]The Greek word Ioudaioi refers specifically here to Jewish religious leaders, and others under their influence, who opposed Jesus in that time; also verses 15, 16, 18

Sabbath. [17]But Jesus answered them, "My Father is working until now, and I am working."

Jesus Is Equal with God

[18]This was why the Jews were seeking all the more to kill him, because not only was he breaking the Sabbath, but he was even calling God his own Father, making himself equal with God.

The Authority of the Son

[19]So Jesus said to them, "Truly, truly, I say to you, the Son can do nothing of his own accord, but only what he sees the Father doing. For whatever the Father[1] does, that the Son does likewise. [20]For the Father loves the Son and shows him all that he himself is doing. And greater works than these will he show him, so that you may marvel. [21]For as the Father raises the dead and gives them life, so also the Son gives life to whom he will. [22]The Father judges no one, but has given all judgment to the Son, [23]that all may honor the Son, just as they honor the Father. Whoever does not honor the Son does not honor the Father who sent him. [24]Truly, truly, I say to you, whoever hears my word and believes him who sent me has eternal life. He does not come into judgment, but has passed from death to life.

[25]"Truly, truly, I say to you, an hour is coming, and is now here, when the dead will hear the voice of the Son of God, and those who hear will live. [26]For as the Father has life in himself, so he has granted the Son also to have life in himself. [27]And he has given him authority to execute judgment, because he is the Son of Man. [28]Do not marvel at this, for an hour is coming when all who are in the tombs will hear his voice [29]and come out, those who have done good to the resurrection of life, and those who have done evil to the resurrection of judgment.

Witnesses to Jesus

[30]"I can do nothing on my own. As I hear, I judge, and my judgment is just, because I seek not my own will but the will of him who sent me. [31]If I alone bear witness about myself, my testimony is not true. [32]There is another who bears witness about me, and I know that the testimony that he bears about me is true. [33]You sent to John, and he has borne witness to the truth. [34]Not that the testimony that I receive is from man, but I say these things so that you may be saved. [35]He was a burning and shining lamp, and you were willing to rejoice for a while in his light. [36]But the testimony that I have is greater than that of John. For the works that the Father has given me to accomplish, the very works that I am doing, bear witness

[1]Greek he

about me that the Father has sent me. ³⁷And the Father who sent me has himself borne witness about me. His voice you have never heard, his form you have never seen, ³⁸and you do not have his word abiding in you, for you do not believe the one whom he has sent. ³⁹You search the Scriptures because you think that in them you have eternal life; and it is they that bear witness about me, ⁴⁰yet you refuse to come to me that you may have life. ⁴¹I do not receive glory from people. ⁴²But I know that you do not have the love of God within you. ⁴³I have come in my Father's name, and you do not receive me. If another comes in his own name, you will receive him. ⁴⁴How can you believe, when you receive glory from one another and do not seek the glory that comes from the only God? ⁴⁵Do not think that I will accuse you to the Father. There is one who accuses you: Moses, on whom you have set your hope. ⁴⁶For if you believed Moses, you would believe me; for he wrote of me. ⁴⁷But if you do not believe his writings, how will you believe my words?"

DAY 6

Jesus Feeds the Five Thousand

6 After this Jesus went away to the other side of the Sea of Galilee, which is the Sea of Tiberias. ²And a large crowd was following him, because they saw the signs that he was doing on the sick. ³Jesus went up on the mountain, and there he sat down with his disciples. ⁴Now the Passover, the feast of the Jews, was at hand. ⁵Lifting up his eyes, then, and seeing that a large crowd was coming toward him, Jesus said to Philip, "Where are we to buy bread, so that these people may eat?" ⁶He said this to test him, for he himself knew what he would do. ⁷Philip answered him, "Two hundred denarii¹ worth of bread would not be enough for each of them to get a little." ⁸One of his disciples, Andrew, Simon Peter's brother, said to him, ⁹"There is a boy here who has five barley loaves and two fish, but what are they for so many?" ¹⁰Jesus said, "Have the people sit down." Now there was much grass in the place. So the men sat down, about five thousand in number. ¹¹Jesus then took the loaves, and when he had given thanks, he distributed them to those who were seated. So also the fish, as much as they wanted. ¹²And when they had eaten their fill, he told his disciples, "Gather up the leftover fragments, that nothing may be lost." ¹³So they gathered them up and filled twelve baskets with fragments from the five barley loaves left by those who had eaten. ¹⁴When the people saw

¹A *denarius* was a day's wage for a laborer

the sign that he had done, they said, "This is indeed the Prophet who is to come into the world!"

[15]Perceiving then that they were about to come and take him by force to make him king, Jesus [a]withdrew again to the mountain by himself.

Jesus Walks on the Water

[16]When evening came, his disciples went down to the sea, [17]got into a boat, and started across the sea to Capernaum. It was now dark, and Jesus had not yet come to them. [18]The sea became rough because a strong wind was blowing. [19]When they had rowed about three or four miles,[1] they saw Jesus walking on the sea and coming near the boat, and they were frightened. [20]But he said to them, "It is I; do not be afraid." [21]Then they were glad to take him into the boat, and immediately the boat was at the land to which they were going.

I Am the Bread of Life

[22]On the next day the crowd that remained on the other side of the sea saw that there had been only one boat there, and that Jesus had not entered the boat with his disciples, but that his disciples had gone away alone. [23]Other boats from Tiberias came near the place where they had eaten the bread after the Lord had given thanks. [24]So when the crowd saw that Jesus was not there, nor his disciples, they themselves got into the boats and went to Capernaum, seeking Jesus.

[25]When they found him on the other side of the sea, they said to him, "Rabbi, when did you come here?" [26]Jesus answered them, "Truly, truly, I say to you, you are seeking me, not because you saw signs, but because you ate your fill of the loaves. [27]Do not work for the food that perishes, but for the food that endures to eternal life, which the Son of Man will give to you. For on him God the Father has set his seal." [28]Then they said to him, "What must we do, to be doing the works of God?" [29]Jesus answered them, "This is the work of God, that you believe in him whom he has sent."

DAY 7

[30]So they said to him, "Then what sign do you do, that we may see and believe you? What work do you perform? [31]Our fathers ate the manna in the wilderness; as it is written, [b]'He gave them bread from heaven to eat.'" [32]Jesus then said to them, "Truly, truly, I say to you, it was not Moses who gave you the bread from heaven, but my Father gives you the true bread

---

[1]Greek *twenty-five or thirty stadia*; a *stadion* was about 607 feet or 185 meters [a]For 6:15-21 see parallels Matt. 14:22-33; Mark 6:45-52 [b]Neh. 9:15

from heaven. [33]For the bread of God is he who comes down from heaven and gives life to the world." [34]They said to him, "Sir, give us this bread always."

[35]Jesus said to them, "I am the bread of life; whoever comes to me shall not hunger, and whoever believes in me shall never thirst. [36]But I said to you that you have seen me and yet do not believe. [37]All that the Father gives me will come to me, and whoever comes to me I will never cast out. [38]For I have come down from heaven, not to do my own will but the will of him who sent me. [39]And this is the will of him who sent me, that I should lose nothing of all that he has given me, but raise it up on the last day. [40]For this is the will of my Father, that everyone who looks on the Son and believes in him should have eternal life, and I will raise him up on the last day."

[41]So the Jews grumbled about him, because he said, "I am the bread that came down from heaven." [42]They said, "Is not this Jesus, the son of Joseph, whose father and mother we know? How does he now say, 'I have come down from heaven'?" [43]Jesus answered them, "Do not grumble among yourselves. [44]No one can come to me unless the Father who sent me draws him. And I will raise him up on the last day. [45]It is written in the Prophets, [a]'And they will all be taught by God.' Everyone who has heard and learned from the Father comes to me—[46]not that anyone has seen the Father except he who is from God; he has seen the Father. [47]Truly, truly, I say to you, whoever believes has eternal life. [48]I am the bread of life. [49]Your fathers ate the manna in the wilderness, and they died. [50]This is the bread that comes down from heaven, so that one may eat of it and not die. [51]I am the living bread that came down from heaven. If anyone eats of this bread, he will live forever. And the bread that I will give for the life of the world is my flesh."

[52]The Jews then disputed among themselves, saying, "How can this man give us his flesh to eat?" [53]So Jesus said to them, "Truly, truly, I say to you, unless you eat the flesh of the Son of Man and drink his blood, you have no life in you. [54]Whoever feeds on my flesh and drinks my blood has eternal life, and I will raise him up on the last day. [55]For my flesh is true food, and my blood is true drink. [56]Whoever feeds on my flesh and drinks my blood abides in me, and I in him. [57]As the living Father sent me, and I live because of the Father, so whoever feeds on me, he also will live because of me. [58]This is the bread that came down from heaven, not like the bread[1] the fathers ate, and died. Whoever feeds on this bread will live forever." [59]Jesus[2] said these things in the synagogue, as he taught at Capernaum.

The Words of Eternal Life

[60]When many of his disciples heard it, they said, "This is a hard saying; who can listen to it?" [61]But Jesus, knowing in himself that his disciples were

[1]Greek lacks *the bread* [2]Greek *He* [a]Isa. 54:13

grumbling about this, said to them, "Do you take offense at this? ⁶²Then what if you were to see the Son of Man ascending to where he was before? ⁶³It is the Spirit who gives life; the flesh is no help at all. The words that I have spoken to you are spirit and life. ⁶⁴But there are some of you who do not believe." (For Jesus knew from the beginning who those were who did not believe, and who it was who would betray him.) ⁶⁵And he said, "This is why I told you that no one can come to me unless it is granted him by the Father."

⁶⁶After this many of his disciples turned back and no longer walked with him. ⁶⁷So Jesus said to the twelve, "Do you want to go away as well?" ⁶⁸Simon Peter answered him, "Lord, to whom shall we go? You have the words of eternal life, ⁶⁹and we have believed, and have come to know, that you are the Holy One of God." ⁷⁰Jesus answered them, "Did I not choose you, the twelve? And yet one of you is a devil." ⁷¹He spoke of Judas the son of Simon Iscariot, for he, one of the twelve, was going to betray him.

DAY 8

Jesus at the Feast of Booths

7 After this Jesus went about in Galilee. He would not go about in Judea, because the Jews¹ were seeking to kill him. ²Now the Jews' Feast of Booths was at hand. ³So his brothers² said to him, "Leave here and go to Judea, that your disciples also may see the works you are doing. ⁴For no one works in secret if he seeks to be known openly. If you do these things, show yourself to the world." ⁵For not even his brothers believed in him. ⁶Jesus said to them, "My time has not yet come, but your time is always here. ⁷The world cannot hate you, but it hates me because I testify about it that its works are evil. ⁸You go up to the feast. I am not³ going up to this feast, for my time has not yet fully come." ⁹After saying this, he remained in Galilee.

¹⁰But after his brothers had gone up to the feast, then he also went up, not publicly but in private. ¹¹The Jews were looking for him at the feast, and saying, "Where is he?" ¹²And there was much muttering about him among the people. While some said, "He is a good man," others said, "No, he is leading the people astray." ¹³Yet for fear of the Jews no one spoke openly of him.

¹⁴About the middle of the feast Jesus went up into the temple and began teaching. ¹⁵The Jews therefore marveled, saying, "How is it that this man has learning,⁴ when he has never studied?" ¹⁶So Jesus answered them, "My teaching is not mine, but his who sent me. ¹⁷If anyone's will is to do God's⁵ will,

¹Or *Judeans*; Greek *Ioudaioi* probably refers here to Jewish religious leaders, and others under their influence, in that time ²Or *brothers and sisters*; also verses 5, 10 ³Some manuscripts add *yet* ⁴Or *this man knows his letters* ⁵Greek *his*

he will know whether the teaching is from God or whether I am speaking on my own authority. ¹⁸The one who speaks on his own authority seeks his own glory; but the one who seeks the glory of him who sent him is true, and in him there is no falsehood. ¹⁹Has not Moses given you the law? Yet none of you keeps the law. Why do you seek to kill me?" ²⁰The crowd answered, "You have a demon! Who is seeking to kill you?" ²¹Jesus answered them, "I did one work, and you all marvel at it. ²²Moses gave you circumcision (not that it is from Moses, but from the fathers), and you circumcise a man on the Sabbath. ²³If on the Sabbath a man receives circumcision, so that the law of Moses may not be broken, are you angry with me because on the Sabbath I made a man's whole body well? ²⁴Do not judge by appearances, but judge with right judgment."

Can This Be the Christ?

²⁵Some of the people of Jerusalem therefore said, "Is not this the man whom they seek to kill? ²⁶And here he is, speaking openly, and they say nothing to him! Can it be that the authorities really know that this is the Christ? ²⁷But we know where this man comes from, and when the Christ appears, no one will know where he comes from." ²⁸So Jesus proclaimed, as he taught in the temple, "You know me, and you know where I come from. But I have not come of my own accord. He who sent me is true, and him you do not know. ²⁹I know him, for I come from him, and he sent me." ³⁰So they were seeking to arrest him, but no one laid a hand on him, because his hour had not yet come. ³¹Yet many of the people believed in him. They said, "When the Christ appears, will he do more signs than this man has done?"

Officers Sent to Arrest Jesus

³²The Pharisees heard the crowd muttering these things about him, and the chief priests and Pharisees sent officers to arrest him. ³³Jesus then said, "I will be with you a little longer, and then I am going to him who sent me. ³⁴You will seek me and you will not find me. Where I am you cannot come." ³⁵The Jews said to one another, "Where does this man intend to go that we will not find him? Does he intend to go to the Dispersion among the Greeks and teach the Greeks? ³⁶What does he mean by saying, 'You will seek me and you will not find me,' and, 'Where I am you cannot come'?"

Rivers of Living Water

³⁷On the last day of the feast, the great day, Jesus stood up and cried out, "If anyone thirsts, let him come to me and drink. ³⁸Whoever believes in me, as⁷ the Scripture has said, 'Out of his heart will flow rivers of living water.'" ³⁹Now this he said about the Spirit, whom those who believed in him were

⁷Or *let him come to me, and let him who believes in me drink. As*

to receive, for as yet the Spirit had not been given, because Jesus was not yet glorified.

Division Among the People

⁴⁰When they heard these words, some of the people said, "This really is the Prophet." ⁴¹Others said, "This is the Christ." But some said, "Is the Christ to come from Galilee? ⁴²Has not the Scripture said that the Christ comes from the offspring of David, and comes from Bethlehem, the village where David was?" ⁴³So there was a division among the people over him. ⁴⁴Some of them wanted to arrest him, but no one laid hands on him.

⁴⁵The officers then came to the chief priests and Pharisees, who said to them, "Why did you not bring him?" ⁴⁶The officers answered, "No one ever spoke like this man!" ⁴⁷The Pharisees answered them, "Have you also been deceived? ⁴⁸Have any of the authorities or the Pharisees believed in him? ⁴⁹But this crowd that does not know the law is accursed." ⁵⁰Nicodemus, who had gone to him before, and who was one of them, said to them, ⁵¹"Does our law judge a man without first giving him a hearing and learning what he does?" ⁵²They replied, "Are you from Galilee too? Search and see that no prophet arises from Galilee."

[THE EARLIEST MANUSCRIPTS DO NOT INCLUDE 7:53–8:11.]¹

DAY 9

The Woman Caught in Adultery

8 ⁵³[[They went each to his own house, ¹but Jesus went to the Mount of Olives. ²Early in the morning he came again to the temple. All the people came to him, and he sat down and taught them. ³The scribes and the Pharisees brought a woman who had been caught in adultery, and placing her in the midst ⁴they said to him, "Teacher, this woman has been caught in the act of adultery. ⁵Now in the Law, Moses commanded us to stone such women. So what do you say?" ⁶This they said to test him, that they might have some charge to bring against him. Jesus bent down and wrote with his finger on the ground. ⁷And as they continued to ask him, he stood up and said to them, "Let him who is without sin among you be the first to throw a stone at her." ⁸And once more he bent down and wrote on the ground. ⁹But when they heard it, they went away one by one, beginning with the older ones, and Jesus was left alone with the woman standing before him. ¹⁰Jesus stood up and said to her, "Woman,

¹Some manuscripts do not include 7:53-8:11; others add the passage here or after 7:36 or after 21:25 or after Luke 21:38, with variations in the text

where are they? Has no one condemned you?" [11]She said, "No one, Lord." And Jesus said, "Neither do I condemn you; go, and from now on sin no more."]]

I Am the Light of the World

[12]Again Jesus spoke to them, saying, "I am the light of the world. Whoever follows me will not walk in darkness, but will have the light of life." [13]So the Pharisees said to him, "You are bearing witness about yourself; your testimony is not true." [14]Jesus answered, "Even if I do bear witness about myself, my testimony is true, for I know where I came from and where I am going, but you do not know where I come from or where I am going. [15]You judge according to the flesh; I judge no one. [16]Yet even if I do judge, my judgment is true, for it is not I alone who judge, but I and the Father[1] who sent me. [17]In your Law it is written that the testimony of two people is true. [18]I am the one who bears witness about myself, and the Father who sent me bears witness about me." [19]They said to him therefore, "Where is your Father?" Jesus answered, "You know neither me nor my Father. If you knew me, you would know my Father also." [20]These words he spoke in the treasury, as he taught in the temple; but no one arrested him, because his hour had not yet come.

[21]So he said to them again, "I am going away, and you will seek me, and you will die in your sin. Where I am going, you cannot come." [22]So the Jews said, "Will he kill himself, since he says, 'Where I am going, you cannot come'?" [23]He said to them, "You are from below; I am from above. You are of this world; I am not of this world. [24]I told you that you would die in your sins, for unless you believe that I am he you will die in your sins." [25]So they said to him, "Who are you?" Jesus said to them, "Just what I have been telling you from the beginning. [26]I have much to say about you and much to judge, but he who sent me is true, and I declare to the world what I have heard from him." [27]They did not understand that he had been speaking to them about the Father. [28]So Jesus said to them, "When you have lifted up the Son of Man, then you will know that I am he, and that I do nothing on my own authority, but speak just as the Father taught me. [29]And he who sent me is with me. He has not left me alone, for I always do the things that are pleasing to him." [30]As he was saying these things, many believed in him.

The Truth Will Set You Free

[31]So Jesus said to the Jews who had believed him, "If you abide in my word, you are truly my disciples, [32]and you will know the truth, and the

---

[1]Some manuscripts *he*

truth will set you free." [33] They answered him, "We are offspring of Abraham and have never been enslaved to anyone. How is it that you say, 'You will become free'?"

[34] Jesus answered them, "Truly, truly, I say to you, everyone who practices sin is a slave to sin. [35] The slave does not remain in the house forever; the son remains forever. [36] So if the Son sets you free, you will be free indeed. [37] I know that you are offspring of Abraham; yet you seek to kill me because my word finds no place in you. [38] I speak of what I have seen with my Father, and you do what you have heard from your father."

You Are of Your Father the Devil

[39] They answered him, "Abraham is our father." Jesus said to them, "If you were Abraham's children, you would be doing the works Abraham did, [40] but now you seek to kill me, a man who has told you the truth that I heard from God. This is not what Abraham did. [41] You are doing the works your father did." They said to him, "We were not born of sexual immorality. We have one Father—even God." [42] Jesus said to them, "If God were your Father, you would love me, for I came from God and I am here. I came not of my own accord, but he sent me. [43] Why do you not understand what I say? It is because you cannot bear to hear my word. [44] You are of your father the devil, and your will is to do your father's desires. He was a murderer from the beginning, and does not stand in the truth, because there is no truth in him. When he lies, he speaks out of his own character, for he is a liar and the father of lies. [45] But because I tell the truth, you do not believe me. [46] Which one of you convicts me of sin? If I tell the truth, why do you not believe me? [47] Whoever is of God hears the words of God. The reason why you do not hear them is that you are not of God."

Before Abraham Was, I Am

[48] The Jews answered him, "Are we not right in saying that you are a Samaritan and have a demon?" [49] Jesus answered, "I do not have a demon, but I honor my Father, and you dishonor me. [50] Yet I do not seek my own glory; there is One who seeks it, and he is the judge. [51] Truly, truly, I say to you, if anyone keeps my word, he will never see death." [52] The Jews said to him, "Now we know that you have a demon! Abraham died, as did the prophets, yet you say, 'If anyone keeps my word, he will never taste death.' [53] Are you greater than our father Abraham, who died? And the prophets died! Who do you make yourself out to be?" [54] Jesus answered, "If I glorify myself, my glory is nothing. It is my Father who glorifies me, of whom you say, 'He is our God.'[1] [55] But you have not known him. I know him. If I were

[1] Some manuscripts *your God*

to say that I do not know him, I would be a liar like you, but I do know him and I keep his word. [56]Your father Abraham rejoiced that he would see my day. He saw it and was glad." [57]So the Jews said to him, "You are not yet fifty years old, and have you seen Abraham?"[1] [58]Jesus said to them, "Truly, truly, I say to you, before Abraham was, I am." [59]So they picked up stones to throw at him, but Jesus hid himself and went out of the temple.

DAY 10

Jesus Heals a Man Born Blind

9 As he passed by, he saw a man blind from birth. [2]And his disciples asked him, "Rabbi, who sinned, this man or his parents, that he was born blind?" [3]Jesus answered, "It was not that this man sinned, or his parents, but that the works of God might be displayed in him. [4]We must work the works of him who sent me while it is day; night is coming, when no one can work. [5]As long as I am in the world, I am the light of the world." [6]Having said these things, he spit on the ground and made mud with the saliva. Then he anointed the man's eyes with the mud [7]and said to him, "Go, wash in the pool of Siloam" (which means Sent). So he went and washed and came back seeing.

[8]The neighbors and those who had seen him before as a beggar were saying, "Is this not the man who used to sit and beg?" [9]Some said, "It is he." Others said, "No, but he is like him." He kept saying, "I am the man." [10]So they said to him, "Then how were your eyes opened?" [11]He answered, "The man called Jesus made mud and anointed my eyes and said to me, 'Go to Siloam and wash.' So I went and washed and received my sight." [12]They said to him, "Where is he?" He said, "I do not know."

[13]They brought to the Pharisees the man who had formerly been blind. [14]Now it was a Sabbath day when Jesus made the mud and opened his eyes. [15]So the Pharisees again asked him how he had received his sight. And he said to them, "He put mud on my eyes, and I washed, and I see." [16]Some of the Pharisees said, "This man is not from God, for he does not keep the Sabbath." But others said, "How can a man who is a sinner do such signs?" And there was a division among them. [17]So they said again to the blind man, "What do you say about him, since he has opened your eyes?" He said, "He is a prophet."

[18]The Jews[2] did not believe that he had been blind and had received his sight, until they called the parents of the man who had received his sight

[1]Some manuscripts *has Abraham seen you?* [2]Greek *Ioudaioi* probably refers here to Jewish religious leaders, and others under their influence, in that time; also verse 22

¹⁹and asked them, "Is this your son, who you say was born blind? How then does he now see?" ²⁰His parents answered, "We know that this is our son and that he was born blind. ²¹But how he now sees we do not know, nor do we know who opened his eyes. Ask him; he is of age. He will speak for himself." ²²(His parents said these things because they feared the Jews, for the Jews had already agreed that if anyone should confess Jesus¹ to be Christ, he was to be put out of the synagogue.) ²³Therefore his parents said, "He is of age; ask him."

²⁴So for the second time they called the man who had been blind and said to him, "Give glory to God. We know that this man is a sinner." ²⁵He answered, "Whether he is a sinner I do not know. One thing I do know, that though I was blind, now I see." ²⁶They said to him, "What did he do to you? How did he open your eyes?" ²⁷He answered them, "I have told you already, and you would not listen. Why do you want to hear it again? Do you also want to become his disciples?" ²⁸And they reviled him, saying, "You are his disciple, but we are disciples of Moses. ²⁹We know that God has spoken to Moses, but as for this man, we do not know where he comes from." ³⁰The man answered, "Why, this is an amazing thing! You do not know where he comes from, and yet he opened my eyes. ³¹We know that God does not listen to sinners, but if anyone is a worshiper of God and does his will, God listens to him. ³²Never since the world began has it been heard that anyone opened the eyes of a man born blind. ³³If this man were not from God, he could do nothing." ³⁴They answered him, "You were born in utter sin, and would you teach us?" And they cast him out.

³⁵Jesus heard that they had cast him out, and having found him he said, "Do you believe in the Son of Man?"² ³⁶He answered, "And who is he, sir, that I may believe in him?" ³⁷Jesus said to him, "You have seen him, and it is he who is speaking to you." ³⁸He said, "Lord, I believe," and he worshiped him. ³⁹Jesus said, "For judgment I came into this world, that those who do not see may see, and those who see may become blind." ⁴⁰Some of the Pharisees near him heard these things, and said to him, "Are we also blind?" ⁴¹Jesus said to them, "If you were blind, you would have no guilt;³ but now that you say, 'We see,' your guilt remains.

¹Greek *him* ²Some manuscripts *the Son of God* ³Greek *you would not have sin*

I Am the Good Shepherd

10 "Truly, truly, I say to you, he who does not enter the sheepfold by the door but climbs in by another way, that man is a thief and a robber. ²But he who enters by the door is the shepherd of the sheep. ³To him the gatekeeper opens. The sheep hear his voice, and he calls his own sheep by name and leads them out. ⁴When he has brought out all his own, he goes before them, and the sheep follow him, for they know his voice. ⁵A stranger they will not follow, but they will flee from him, for they do not know the voice of strangers." ⁶This figure of speech Jesus used with them, but they did not understand what he was saying to them.

⁷So Jesus again said to them, "Truly, truly, I say to you, I am the door of the sheep. ⁸All who came before me are thieves and robbers, but the sheep did not listen to them. ⁹I am the door. If anyone enters by me, he will be saved and will go in and out and find pasture. ¹⁰The thief comes only to steal and kill and destroy. I came that they may have life and have it abundantly. ¹¹I am the good shepherd. The good shepherd lays down his life for the sheep. ¹²He who is a hired hand and not a shepherd, who does not own the sheep, sees the wolf coming and leaves the sheep and flees, and the wolf snatches them and scatters them. ¹³He flees because he is a hired hand and cares nothing for the sheep. ¹⁴I am the good shepherd. I know my own and my own know me, ¹⁵just as the Father knows me and I know the Father; and I lay down my life for the sheep. ¹⁶And I have other sheep that are not of this fold. I must bring them also, and they will listen to my voice. So there will be one flock, one shepherd. ¹⁷For this reason the Father loves me, because I lay down my life that I may take it up again. ¹⁸No one takes it from me, but I lay it down of my own accord. I have authority to lay it down, and I have authority to take it up again. This charge I have received from my Father."

¹⁹There was again a division among the Jews because of these words. ²⁰Many of them said, "He has a demon, and is insane; why listen to him?" ²¹Others said, "These are not the words of one who is oppressed by a demon. Can a demon open the eyes of the blind?"

I and the Father Are One

²²At that time the Feast of Dedication took place at Jerusalem. It

was winter, [23]and Jesus was walking in the temple, in the colonnade of Solomon. [24]So the Jews gathered around him and said to him, "How long will you keep us in suspense? If you are the Christ, tell us plainly." [25]Jesus answered them, "I told you, and you do not believe. The works that I do in my Father's name bear witness about me, [26]but you do not believe because you are not among my sheep. [27]My sheep hear my voice, and I know them, and they follow me. [28]I give them eternal life, and they will never perish, and no one will snatch them out of my hand. [29]My Father, who has given them to me,[1] is greater than all, and no one is able to snatch them out of the Father's hand. [30]I and the Father are one."

[31]The Jews picked up stones again to stone him. [32]Jesus answered them, "I have shown you many good works from the Father; for which of them are you going to stone me?" [33]The Jews answered him, "It is not for a good work that we are going to stone you but for blasphemy, because you, being a man, make yourself God." [34]Jesus answered them, "Is it not written in your Law, [a]'I said, you are gods'? [35]If he called them gods to whom the word of God came—and Scripture cannot be broken—[36]do you say of him whom the Father consecrated and sent into the world, 'You are blaspheming,' because I said, 'I am the Son of God'? [37]If I am not doing the works of my Father, then do not believe me; [38]but if I do them, even though you do not believe me, believe the works, that you may know and understand that the Father is in me and I am in the Father." [39]Again they sought to arrest him, but he escaped from their hands.

[40]He went away again across the Jordan to the place where John had been baptizing at first, and there he remained. [41]And many came to him. And they said, "John did no sign, but everything that John said about this man was true." [42]And many believed in him there.

DAY 13

The Death of Lazarus

11 Now a certain man was ill, Lazarus of Bethany, the village of Mary and her sister Martha. [2]It was Mary who anointed the Lord with ointment and wiped his feet with her hair, whose brother Lazarus was ill. [3]So the sisters sent to him, saying, "Lord, he whom you love is ill." [4]But when Jesus heard it he said, "This illness does not lead to death. It is for the glory of God, so that the Son of God may be glorified through it."

[1]Some manuscripts *What my Father has given to me* [a]Ps. 82:6

⁵Now Jesus loved Martha and her sister and Lazarus. ⁶So, when he heard that Lazarus*¹* was ill, he stayed two days longer in the place where he was. ⁷Then after this he said to the disciples, "Let us go to Judea again." ⁸The disciples said to him, "Rabbi, the Jews were just now seeking to stone you, and are you going there again?" ⁹Jesus answered, "Are there not twelve hours in the day? If anyone walks in the day, he does not stumble, because he sees the light of this world. ¹⁰But if anyone walks in the night, he stumbles, because the light is not in him." ¹¹After saying these things, he said to them, "Our friend Lazarus has fallen asleep, but I go to awaken him." ¹²The disciples said to him, "Lord, if he has fallen asleep, he will recover." ¹³Now Jesus had spoken of his death, but they thought that he meant taking rest in sleep. ¹⁴Then Jesus told them plainly, "Lazarus has died, ¹⁵and for your sake I am glad that I was not there, so that you may believe. But let us go to him." ¹⁶So Thomas, called the Twin,*²* said to his fellow disciples, "Let us also go, that we may die with him."

I Am the Resurrection and the Life

¹⁷Now when Jesus came, he found that Lazarus had already been in the tomb four days. ¹⁸Bethany was near Jerusalem, about two miles*³* off, ¹⁹and many of the Jews had come to Martha and Mary to console them concerning their brother. ²⁰So when Martha heard that Jesus was coming, she went and met him, but Mary remained seated in the house. ²¹Martha said to Jesus, "Lord, if you had been here, my brother would not have died. ²²But even now I know that whatever you ask from God, God will give you." ²³Jesus said to her, "Your brother will rise again." ²⁴Martha said to him, "I know that he will rise again in the resurrection on the last day." ²⁵Jesus said to her, "I am the resurrection and the life.*⁴* Whoever believes in me, though he die, yet shall he live, ²⁶and everyone who lives and believes in me shall never die. Do you believe this?" ²⁷She said to him, "Yes, Lord; I believe that you are the Christ, the Son of God, who is coming into the world."

Jesus Weeps

²⁸When she had said this, she went and called her sister Mary, saying in private, "The Teacher is here and is calling for you." ²⁹And when she heard it, she rose quickly and went to him. ³⁰Now Jesus had not yet come into the village, but was still in the place where Martha had met him. ³¹When the Jews who were with her in the house, consoling her, saw Mary rise quickly and go out, they followed her, supposing that she was going to the tomb to weep there. ³²Now when Mary came to where Jesus was and saw him,

¹Greek *he*; also verse 17 ²Greek *Didymus* ³Greek *fifteen stadia*; a *stadion* was about 607 feet or 185 meters ⁴Some manuscripts omit *and the life*

she fell at his feet, saying to him, "Lord, if you had been here, my brother would not have died." [33]When Jesus saw her weeping, and the Jews who had come with her also weeping, he was deeply moved[/] in his spirit and greatly troubled. [34]And he said, "Where have you laid him?" They said to him, "Lord, come and see." [35]Jesus wept. [36]So the Jews said, "See how he loved him!" [37]But some of them said, "Could not he who opened the eyes of the blind man also have kept this man from dying?"

Jesus Raises Lazarus

[38]Then Jesus, deeply moved again, came to the tomb. It was a cave, and a stone lay against it. [39]Jesus said, "Take away the stone." Martha, the sister of the dead man, said to him, "Lord, by this time there will be an odor, for he has been dead four days." [40]Jesus said to her, "Did I not tell you that if you believed you would see the glory of God?" [41]So they took away the stone. And Jesus lifted up his eyes and said, "Father, I thank you that you have heard me. [42]I knew that you always hear me, but I said this on account of the people standing around, that they may believe that you sent me." [43]When he had said these things, he cried out with a loud voice, "Lazarus, come out." [44]The man who had died came out, his hands and feet bound with linen strips, and his face wrapped with a cloth. Jesus said to them, "Unbind him, and let him go."

The Plot to Kill Jesus

[45]Many of the Jews therefore, who had come with Mary and had seen what he did, believed in him, [46]but some of them went to the Pharisees and told them what Jesus had done. [47]So the chief priests and the Pharisees gathered the council and said, "What are we to do? For this man performs many signs. [48]If we let him go on like this, everyone will believe in him, and the Romans will come and take away both our place and our nation." [49]But one of them, Caiaphas, who was high priest that year, said to them, "You know nothing at all. [50]Nor do you understand that it is better for you that one man should die for the people, not that the whole nation should perish." [51]He did not say this of his own accord, but being high priest that year he prophesied that Jesus would die for the nation, [52]and not for the nation only, but also to gather into one the children of God who are scattered abroad. [53]So from that day on they made plans to put him to death.

[54]Jesus therefore no longer walked openly among the Jews, but went from there to the region near the wilderness, to a town called Ephraim, and there he stayed with the disciples.

[/]Or was indignant; also verse 38

⁵⁵Now the Passover of the Jews was at hand, and many went up from the country to Jerusalem before the Passover to purify themselves. ⁵⁶They were looking for¹ Jesus and saying to one another as they stood in the temple, "What do you think? That he will not come to the feast at all?" ⁵⁷Now the chief priests and the Pharisees had given orders that if anyone knew where he was, he should let them know, so that they might arrest him.

DAY 14

Mary Anoints Jesus at Bethany

12Six days before the Passover, Jesus therefore came to Bethany, where Lazarus was, whom Jesus had raised from the dead. ²So they gave a dinner for him there. Martha served, and Lazarus was one of those reclining with him at table. ³Mary therefore took a pound² of expensive ointment made from pure nard, and anointed the feet of Jesus and wiped his feet with her hair. The house was filled with the fragrance of the perfume. ⁴But Judas Iscariot, one of his disciples (he who was about to betray him), said, ⁵"Why was this ointment not sold for three hundred denarii³ and given to the poor?" ⁶He said this, not because he cared about the poor, but because he was a thief, and having charge of the moneybag he used to help himself to what was put into it. ⁷Jesus said, "Leave her alone, so that she may keep it⁴ for the day of my burial. ⁸For the poor you always have with you but you do not always have me."

The Plot to Kill Lazarus

⁹When the large crowd of the Jews learned that Jesus⁵ was there, they came, not only on account of him but also to see Lazarus, whom he had raised from the dead. ¹⁰So the chief priests made plans to put Lazarus to death as well, ¹¹because on account of him many of the Jews were going away and believing in Jesus.

The Triumphal Entry

¹²The next day ᵃthe large crowd that had come to the feast heard that Jesus was coming to Jerusalem. ¹³So they took branches of palm trees and went out to meet him, crying out, "Hosanna! Blessed is he who comes in the name of the Lord, even the King of Israel!" ¹⁴And Jesus found a young donkey and sat on it, just as it is written,

¹⁵ ᵇ"Fear not, daughter of Zion;

¹Greek were seeking for ²Greek litra; a litra (or Roman pound) was equal to about 11 1/2 ounces or 327 grams ³A denarius was a day's wage for a laborer ⁴Or Leave her alone; she intended to keep it ⁵Greek he ᵃFor 12:12-15 see parallels Matt. 21:4-9; Mark 11:7-10; Luke 19:35-38 ᵇZech. 9:9

> behold, your king is coming,
>> sitting on a donkey's colt!"

[16]His disciples did not understand these things at first, but when Jesus was glorified, then they remembered that these things had been written about him and had been done to him. [17]The crowd that had been with him when he called Lazarus out of the tomb and raised him from the dead continued to bear witness. [18]The reason why the crowd went to meet him was that they heard he had done this sign. [19]So the Pharisees said to one another, "You see that you are gaining nothing. Look, the world has gone after him."

Some Greeks Seek Jesus

Now among those who went up to worship at the feast were some Greeks. [21]So these came to Philip, who was from Bethsaida in Galilee, and asked him, "Sir, we wish to see Jesus." [22]Philip went and told Andrew; Andrew and Philip went and told Jesus. [23]And Jesus answered them, "The hour has come for the Son of Man to be glorified. [24]Truly, truly, I say to you, unless a grain of wheat falls into the earth and dies, it remains alone; but if it dies, it bears much fruit. [25]Whoever loves his life loses it, and whoever hates his life in this world will keep it for eternal life. [26]If anyone serves me, he must follow me; and where I am, there will my servant be also. If anyone serves me, the Father will honor him.

The Son of Man Must Be Lifted Up

[27]"Now is my soul troubled. And what shall I say? 'Father, save me from this hour'? But for this purpose I have come to this hour. [28]Father, glorify your name." Then a voice came from heaven: "I have glorified it, and I will glorify it again." [29]The crowd that stood there and heard it said that it had thundered. Others said, "An angel has spoken to him." [30]Jesus answered, "This voice has come for your sake, not mine. [31]Now is the judgment of this world; now will the ruler of this world be cast out. [32]And I, when I am lifted up from the earth, will draw all people to myself." [33]He said this to show by what kind of death he was going to die. [34]So the crowd answered him, "We have heard from the Law that the Christ remains forever. How can you say that the Son of Man must be lifted up? Who is this Son of Man?" [35]So Jesus said to them, "The light is among you for a little while longer. Walk while you have the light, lest darkness overtake you. The one who walks in the darkness does not know where he is going. [36]While you have the light, believe in the light, that you may become sons of light."

The Unbelief of the People

When Jesus had said these things, he departed and hid himself from them. [37]Though he had done so many signs before them, they still did not believe in him, [38]so that the word spoken by the prophet Isaiah might be fulfilled:

[a]"Lord, who has believed what he heard from us,
    and to whom has the arm of the Lord
      been revealed?"

[39]Therefore they could not believe. For again Isaiah said,

[40][b]"He has blinded their eyes
    and hardened their heart,
  lest they see with their eyes,
    and understand with their heart, and turn,
    and I would heal them."

[41]Isaiah said these things because he saw his glory and spoke of him. [42]Nevertheless, many even of the authorities believed in him, but for fear of the Pharisees they did not confess it, so that they would not be put out of the synagogue; [43]for they loved the glory that comes from man more than the glory that comes from God.

Jesus Came to Save the World

[44]And Jesus cried out and said, "Whoever believes in me, believes not in me but in him who sent me. [45]And whoever sees me sees him who sent me. [46]I have come into the world as light, so that whoever believes in me may not remain in darkness. [47]If anyone hears my words and does not keep them, I do not judge him; for I did not come to judge the world but to save the world. [48]The one who rejects me and does not receive my words has a judge; the word that I have spoken will judge him on the last day. [49]For I have not spoken on my own authority, but the Father who sent me has himself given me a commandment—what to say and what to speak. [50]And I know that his commandment is eternal life. What I say, therefore, I say as the Father has told me."

[a]Isa. 53:1 [b]Isa. 6:10

DAY 15

Jesus Washes the Disciples' Feet

13 Now before the Feast of the Passover, when Jesus knew that his hour had come to depart out of this world to the Father, having loved his own who were in the world, he loved them to the end. [2]During supper, when the devil had already put it into the heart of Judas Iscariot, Simon's son, to betray him, [3]Jesus, knowing that the Father had given all things into his hands, and that he had come from God and was going back to God, [4]rose from supper. He laid aside his outer garments, and taking a towel, tied it around his waist. [5]Then he poured water into a basin and began to wash the disciples' feet and to wipe them with the towel that was wrapped around him. [6]He came to Simon Peter, who said to him, "Lord, do you wash my feet?" [7]Jesus answered him, "What I am doing you do not understand now, but afterward you will understand." [8]Peter said to him, "You shall never wash my feet." Jesus answered him, "If I do not wash you, you have no share with me." [9]Simon Peter said to him, "Lord, not my feet only but also my hands and my head!" [10]Jesus said to him, "The one who has bathed does not need to wash, except for his feet,[1] but is completely clean. And you[2] are clean, but not every one of you." [11]For he knew who was to betray him; that was why he said, "Not all of you are clean."

[12]When he had washed their feet and put on his outer garments and resumed his place, he said to them, "Do you understand what I have done to you? [13]You call me Teacher and Lord, and you are right, for so I am. [14]If I then, your Lord and Teacher, have washed your feet, you also ought to wash one another's feet. [15]For I have given you an example, that you also should do just as I have done to you. [16]Truly, truly, I say to you, a servant[3] is not greater than his master, nor is a messenger greater than the one who sent him. [17]If you know these things, blessed are you if you do them. [18]I am not speaking of all of you; I know whom I have chosen. But the Scripture will be fulfilled,[4] [a]'He who ate my bread has lifted his heel against me.' [19]I am telling you this now, before it takes place, that when it does take place you may believe that I am he. [20]Truly, truly, I say to you, whoever receives the one I send receives me, and whoever receives me receives the one who sent me."

One of You Will Betray Me

[21]After saying these things, Jesus was troubled in his spirit, and testified,

---

[1]Some manuscripts omit *except for his feet* [2]The Greek words for *you* in this verse are plural [3]Greek *bondservant* [4]Greek *But in order that the Scripture may be fulfilled* [a]Ps. 41:9

"Truly, truly, I say to you, one of you will betray me." [22]The disciples looked at one another, uncertain of whom he spoke. [23]One of his disciples, whom Jesus loved, was reclining at table at Jesus' side,[1] [24]so Simon Peter motioned to him to ask Jesus[2] of whom he was speaking. [25]So that disciple, leaning back against Jesus, said to him, "Lord, who is it?" [26]Jesus answered, "It is he to whom I will give this morsel of bread when I have dipped it." So when he had dipped the morsel, he gave it to Judas, the son of Simon Iscariot. [27]Then after he had taken the morsel, Satan entered into him. Jesus said to him, "What you are going to do, do quickly." [28]Now no one at the table knew why he said this to him. [29]Some thought that, because Judas had the moneybag, Jesus was telling him, "Buy what we need for the feast," or that he should give something to the poor. [30]So, after receiving the morsel of bread, he immediately went out. And it was night.

A New Commandment

[31]When he had gone out, Jesus said, "Now is the Son of Man glorified, and God is glorified in him. [32]If God is glorified in him, God will also glorify him in himself, and glorify him at once. [33]Little children, yet a little while I am with you. You will seek me, and just as I said to the Jews, so now I also say to you, 'Where I am going you cannot come.' [34]A new commandment I give to you, that you love one another: just as I have loved you, you also are to love one another. [35]By this all people will know that you are my disciples, if you have love for one another."

Jesus Foretells Peter's Denial

[36]Simon Peter said to him, "Lord, where are you going?" Jesus answered him, "Where I am going you cannot follow me now, but you will follow afterward." [37]Peter said to him, "Lord, why can I not follow you now? I will lay down my life for you." [38]Jesus answered, "Will you lay down your life for me? Truly, truly, I say to you, the rooster will not crow till you have denied me three times.

DAY 16

I Am the Way, and the Truth, and the Life

14 "Let not your hearts be troubled. Believe in God;[3] believe also in me. [2]In my Father's house are many rooms. If it were not so, would I have

[1]Greek *in the bosom of Jesus* [2]Greek lacks *Jesus* [3]Or *You believe in God*

79

told you that I go to prepare a place for you?[1] [3]And if I go and prepare a place for you, I will come again and will take you to myself, that where I am you may be also. [4]And you know the way to where I am going."[2] [5]Thomas said to him, "Lord, we do not know where you are going. How can we know the way?" [6]Jesus said to him, "I am the way, and the truth, and the life. No one comes to the Father except through me. [7]If you had known me, you would have known my Father also.[3] From now on you do know him and have seen him."

[8]Philip said to him, "Lord, show us the Father, and it is enough for us." [9]Jesus said to him, "Have I been with you so long, and you still do not know me, Philip? Whoever has seen me has seen the Father. How can you say, 'Show us the Father'? [10]Do you not believe that I am in the Father and the Father is in me? The words that I say to you I do not speak on my own authority, but the Father who dwells in me does his works. [11]Believe me that I am in the Father and the Father is in me, or else believe on account of the works themselves.

[12]"Truly, truly, I say to you, whoever believes in me will also do the works that I do; and greater works than these will he do, because I am going to the Father. [13]Whatever you ask in my name, this I will do, that the Father may be glorified in the Son. [14]If you ask me[4] anything in my name, I will do it.

DAY 17

Jesus Promises the Holy Spirit

[15]"If you love me, you will keep my commandments. [16]And I will ask the Father, and he will give you another Helper,[5] to be with you forever, [17]even the Spirit of truth, whom the world cannot receive, because it neither sees him nor knows him. You know him, for he dwells with you and will be[6] in you.

[18]"I will not leave you as orphans; I will come to you. [19]Yet a little while and the world will see me no more, but you will see me. Because I live, you also will live. [20]In that day you will know that I am in my Father, and you in me, and I in you. [21]Whoever has my commandments and keeps them, he it is who loves me. And he who loves me will be loved by my Father, and I will love him and manifest myself to him." [22]Judas (not Iscariot) said to him, "Lord, how is it that you will manifest yourself to us, and not to the world?" [23]Jesus answered him, "If anyone loves me, he will keep my word,

[1]Or *In my Father's house are many rooms; if it were not so, I would have told you; for I go to prepare a place for you* [2]Some manuscripts *Where I am going you know, and the way you know* [3]Or *If you know me, you will know my Father also,* or *If you have known me, you will know my Father also* [4]Some manuscripts omit *me* [5]Or *Advocate,* or *Counselor;* also 14:26; 15:26; 16:7 [6]Some manuscripts *and is*

and my Father will love him, and we will come to him and make our home with him. ²⁴Whoever does not love me does not keep my words. And the word that you hear is not mine but the Father's who sent me.

²⁵"These things I have spoken to you while I am still with you. ²⁶But the Helper, the Holy Spirit, whom the Father will send in my name, he will teach you all things and bring to your remembrance all that I have said to you. ²⁷Peace I leave with you; my peace I give to you. Not as the world gives do I give to you. Let not your hearts be troubled, neither let them be afraid. ²⁸You heard me say to you, 'I am going away, and I will come to you.' If you loved me, you would have rejoiced, because I am going to the Father, for the Father is greater than I. ²⁹And now I have told you before it takes place, so that when it does take place you may believe. ³⁰I will no longer talk much with you, for the ruler of this world is coming. He has no claim on me, ³¹but I do as the Father has commanded me, so that the world may know that I love the Father. Rise, let us go from here.

DAY 18

I Am the True Vine

15 "I am the true vine, and my Father is the vinedresser. ²Every branch in me that does not bear fruit he takes away, and every branch that does bear fruit he prunes, that it may bear more fruit. ³Already you are clean because of the word that I have spoken to you. ⁴Abide in me, and I in you. As the branch cannot bear fruit by itself, unless it abides in the vine, neither can you, unless you abide in me. ⁵I am the vine; you are the branches. Whoever abides in me and I in him, he it is that bears much fruit, for apart from me you can do nothing. ⁶If anyone does not abide in me he is thrown away like a branch and withers; and the branches are gathered, thrown into the fire, and burned. ⁷If you abide in me, and my words abide in you, ask whatever you wish, and it will be done for you. ⁸By this my Father is glorified, that you bear much fruit and so prove to be my disciples. ⁹As the Father has loved me, so have I loved you. Abide in my love. ¹⁰If you keep my commandments, you will abide in my love, just as I have kept my Father's commandments and abide in his love. ¹¹These things I have spoken to you, that my joy may be in you, and that your joy may be full.

¹²"This is my commandment, that you love one another as I have loved you. ¹³Greater love has no one than this, that someone lay down his life

for his friends. [14]You are my friends if you do what I command you. [15]No longer do I call you servants,[1] for the servant does not know what his master is doing; but I have called you friends, for all that I have heard from my Father I have made known to you. [16]You did not choose me, but I chose you and appointed you that you should go and bear fruit and that your fruit should abide, so that whatever you ask the Father in my name, he may give it to you. [17]These things I command you, so that you will love one another.

The Hatred of the World

[18]"If the world hates you, know that it has hated me before it hated you. [19]If you were of the world, the world would love you as its own; but because you are not of the world, but I chose you out of the world, therefore the world hates you. [20]Remember the word that I said to you: 'A servant is not greater than his master.' If they persecuted me, they will also persecute you. If they kept my word, they will also keep yours. [21]But all these things they will do to you on account of my name, because they do not know him who sent me. [22]If I had not come and spoken to them, they would not have been guilty of sin,[2] but now they have no excuse for their sin. [23]Whoever hates me hates my Father also. [24]If I had not done among them the works that no one else did, they would not be guilty of sin, but now they have seen and hated both me and my Father. [25]But the word that is written in their Law must be fulfilled: [a]'They hated me without a cause.'

[26]"But when the Helper comes, whom I will send to you from the Father, the Spirit of truth, who proceeds from the Father, he will bear witness about me. [27]And you also will bear witness, because you have been with me from the beginning.

DAY 19

16[1]"I have said all these things to you to keep you from falling away. [2]They will put you out of the synagogues. Indeed, the hour is coming when whoever kills you will think he is offering service to God. [3]And they will do these things because they have not known the Father, nor me. [4]But I have said these things to you, that when their hour comes you may remember that I told them to you.

[1]Greek *bondservants*; likewise for *servant* later in this verse and in verse 20 [2]Greek *they would not have sin*; also verse 24 [a]Ps. 35:19 or 69:4

The Work of the Holy Spirit

"I did not say these things to you from the beginning, because I was with you. ⁵But now I am going to him who sent me, and none of you asks me, 'Where are you going?' ⁶But because I have said these things to you, sorrow has filled your heart. ⁷Nevertheless, I tell you the truth: it is to your advantage that I go away, for if I do not go away, the Helper will not come to you. But if I go, I will send him to you. ⁸And when he comes, he will convict the world concerning sin and righteousness and judgment: ⁹concerning sin, because they do not believe in me; ¹⁰concerning righteousness, because I go to the Father, and you will see me no longer; ¹¹concerning judgment, because the ruler of this world is judged.

¹²"I still have many things to say to you, but you cannot bear them now. ¹³When the Spirit of truth comes, he will guide you into all the truth, for he will not speak on his own authority, but whatever he hears he will speak, and he will declare to you the things that are to come. ¹⁴He will glorify me, for he will take what is mine and declare it to you. ¹⁵All that the Father has is mine; therefore I said that he will take what is mine and declare it to you.

DAY 20

Your Sorrow Will Turn into Joy

¹⁶"A little while, and you will see me no longer; and again a little while, and you will see me." ¹⁷So some of his disciples said to one another, "What is this that he says to us, 'A little while, and you will not see me, and again a little while, and you will see me'; and, 'because I am going to the Father'?" ¹⁸So they were saying, "What does he mean by 'a little while'? We do not know what he is talking about." ¹⁹Jesus knew that they wanted to ask him, so he said to them, "Is this what you are asking yourselves, what I meant by saying, 'A little while and you will not see me, and again a little while and you will see me'? ²⁰Truly, truly, I say to you, you will weep and lament, but the world will rejoice. You will be sorrowful, but your sorrow will turn into joy. ²¹When a woman is giving birth, she has sorrow because her hour has come, but when she has delivered the baby, she no longer remembers the anguish, for joy that a human being has been born into the world. ²²So also you have sorrow now, but I will see you again, and your hearts will rejoice, and no one will take your joy from you. ²³In that day you will ask nothing of me. Truly, truly, I say to you, whatever you ask of the Father in

my name, he will give it to you. [24]Until now you have asked nothing in my name. Ask, and you will receive, that your joy may be full.

I Have Overcome the World

[25]"I have said these things to you in figures of speech. The hour is coming when I will no longer speak to you in figures of speech but will tell you plainly about the Father. [26]In that day you will ask in my name, and I do not say to you that I will ask the Father on your behalf; [27]for the Father himself loves you, because you have loved me and have believed that I came from God.[1] [28]I came from the Father and have come into the world, and now I am leaving the world and going to the Father."

[29]His disciples said, "Ah, now you are speaking plainly and not using figurative speech! [30]Now we know that you know all things and do not need anyone to question you; this is why we believe that you came from God." [31]Jesus answered them, "Do you now believe? [32]Behold, the hour is coming, indeed it has come, when you will be scattered, each to his own home, and will leave me alone. Yet I am not alone, for the Father is with me. [33]I have said these things to you, that in me you may have peace. In the world you will have tribulation. But take heart; I have overcome the world."

DAY 21

The High Priestly Prayer

17When Jesus had spoken these words, he lifted up his eyes to heaven, and said, "Father, the hour has come; glorify your Son that the Son may glorify you, [2]since you have given him authority over all flesh, to give eternal life to all whom you have given him. [3]And this is eternal life, that they know you, the only true God, and Jesus Christ whom you have sent. [4]I glorified you on earth, having accomplished the work that you gave me to do. [5]And now, Father, glorify me in your own presence with the glory that I had with you before the world existed.

[6]"I have manifested your name to the people whom you gave me out of the world. Yours they were, and you gave them to me, and they have kept your word. [7]Now they know that everything that you have given me is from you. [8]For I have given them the words that you gave me, and they have received them and have come to know in truth that I came from you; and they have believed that you sent me. [9]I am praying for them. I am not praying for the world but for those whom you have given me, for they

[1]Some manuscripts *from the Father*

are yours. [10]All mine are yours, and yours are mine, and I am glorified in them. [11]And I am no longer in the world, but they are in the world, and I am coming to you. Holy Father, keep them in your name, which you have given me, that they may be one, even as we are one. [12]While I was with them, I kept them in your name, which you have given me. I have guarded them, and not one of them has been lost except the son of destruction, that the Scripture might be fulfilled. [13]But now I am coming to you, and these things I speak in the world, that they may have my joy fulfilled in themselves. [14]I have given them your word, and the world has hated them because they are not of the world, just as I am not of the world. [15]I do not ask that you take them out of the world, but that you keep them from the evil one.[1][16]They are not of the world, just as I am not of the world. [17]Sanctify them[2] in the truth; your word is truth. [18]As you sent me into the world, so I have sent them into the world. [19]And for their sake I consecrate myself,[3] that they also may be sanctified[4] in truth.

[20]"I do not ask for these only, but also for those who will believe in me through their word, [21]that they may all be one, just as you, Father, are in me, and I in you, that they also may be in us, so that the world may believe that you have sent me. [22]The glory that you have given me I have given to them, that they may be one even as we are one, [23]I in them and you in me, that they may become perfectly one, so that the world may know that you sent me and loved them even as you loved me. [24]Father, I desire that they also, whom you have given me, may be with me where I am, to see my glory that you have given me because you loved me before the foundation of the world. [25]O righteous Father, even though the world does not know you, I know you, and these know that you have sent me. [26]I made known to them your name, and I will continue to make it known, that the love with which you have loved me may be in them, and I in them."

DAY 22

Betrayal and Arrest of Jesus

18 When Jesus had spoken these words, he went out with his disciples across the brook Kidron, where there was a garden, which he and his disciples entered. [2]Now Judas, who betrayed him, also knew the place, for Jesus often met there with his disciples. [3][a] So Judas, having procured a band of soldiers and some officers from the chief priests and the Pharisees, went there with lanterns and torches and weapons. [4]Then

[1]Or *from evil* [2]Greek *Set them apart* (for holy service to God) [3]Or *I sanctify myself*; or *I set myself apart* (for holy service to God) [4]Greek *may be set apart* (for holy service to God) [a]For 18:3-11 see parallels Matt. 26:47-56; Mark 14:43-50; Luke 22:47-53

Jesus, knowing all that would happen to him, came forward and said to them, "Whom do you seek?" [5]They answered him, "Jesus of Nazareth." Jesus said to them, "I am he."[1] Judas, who betrayed him, was standing with them. [6]When Jesus[2] said to them, "I am he," they drew back and fell to the ground. [7]So he asked them again, "Whom do you seek?" And they said, "Jesus of Nazareth." [8]Jesus answered, "I told you that I am he. So, if you seek me, let these men go." [9]This was to fulfill the word that he had spoken: "Of those whom you gave me I have lost not one." [10]Then Simon Peter, having a sword, drew it and struck the high priest's servant[3] and cut off his right ear. (The servant's name was Malchus.) [11]So Jesus said to Peter, "Put your sword into its sheath; shall I not drink the cup that the Father has given me?"

Jesus Faces Annas and Caiaphas

[12]"So the band of soldiers and their captain and the officers of the Jews[4] arrested Jesus and bound him. [13]First they led him to Annas, for he was the father-in-law of Caiaphas, who was high priest that year. [14]It was Caiaphas who had advised the Jews that it would be expedient that one man should die for the people.

DAY 23

Peter Denies Jesus

[15]Simon Peter followed Jesus, and so did another disciple. Since that disciple was known to the high priest, he entered with Jesus into the courtyard of the high priest, [16 a] but Peter stood outside at the door. So the other disciple, who was known to the high priest, went out and spoke to the servant girl who kept watch at the door, and brought Peter in. [17]The servant girl at the door said to Peter, "You also are not one of this man's disciples, are you?" He said, "I am not." [18]Now the servants[5] and officers had made a charcoal fire, because it was cold, and they were standing and warming themselves. Peter also was with them, standing and warming himself.

The High Priest Questions Jesus

[19]The high priest then questioned Jesus about his disciples and his teaching. [20]Jesus answered him, "I have spoken openly to the world. I have always taught in synagogues and in the temple, where all Jews come

[1]Greek *I am*; also verses 6, 8 [2]Greek *he* [3]Or *bondservant*; twice in this verse [4]Greek *Ioudaioi* probably refers here to Jewish religious leaders, and others under their influence, in that time; also verses 14, 31, 36, 38 [5]Or *bondservants*; also verse 26 [a]For 18:16-18 see parallels Matt. 26:69, 70; Mark 14:66-68; Luke 22:55-57

together. I have said nothing in secret. ²¹Why do you ask me? Ask those who have heard me what I said to them; they know what I said." ²²When he had said these things, one of the officers standing by struck Jesus with his hand, saying, "Is that how you answer the high priest?" ²³Jesus answered him, "If what I said is wrong, bear witness about the wrong; but if what I said is right, why do you strike me?" ²⁴Annas then sent him bound to Caiaphas the high priest.

Peter Denies Jesus Again

^{25 a} Now Simon Peter was standing and warming himself. So they said to him, "You also are not one of his disciples, are you?" He denied it and said, "I am not." ²⁶One of the servants of the high priest, a relative of the man whose ear Peter had cut off, asked, "Did I not see you in the garden with him?" ²⁷Peter again denied it, and at once a rooster crowed.

DAY 24

Jesus Before Pilate

²⁸Then they led Jesus from the house of Caiaphas to the governor's headquarters.¹ It was early morning. They themselves did not enter the governor's headquarters, so that they would not be defiled, but could eat the Passover. ^{29 b} So Pilate went outside to them and said, "What accusation do you bring against this man?" ³⁰They answered him, "If this man were not doing evil, we would not have delivered him over to you." ³¹Pilate said to them, "Take him yourselves and judge him by your own law." The Jews said to him, "It is not lawful for us to put anyone to death." ³²This was to fulfill the word that Jesus had spoken to show by what kind of death he was going to die.

My Kingdom Is Not of This World

³³So Pilate entered his headquarters again and called Jesus and said to him, "Are you the King of the Jews?" ³⁴Jesus answered, "Do you say this of your own accord, or did others say it to you about me?" ³⁵Pilate answered, "Am I a Jew? Your own nation and the chief priests have delivered you over to me. What have you done?" ³⁶Jesus answered, "My kingdom is not of this world. If my kingdom were of this world, my servants would have been fighting, that I might not be delivered over to the Jews. But my kingdom is not from the world." ³⁷Then Pilate said to him, "So you are a

¹Greek *the praetorium* ^aFor 18:25-27 see parallels Matt. 26:71-75; Mark 14:69-72; Luke 22:58-62 ^bFor 18:29-38 see parallels Matt. 27:11-14; Mark 15:1-5; Luke 23:1-3

king?" Jesus answered, "You say that I am a king. For this purpose I was born and for this purpose I have come into the world—to bear witness to the truth. Everyone who is of the truth listens to my voice." [38]Pilate said to him, "What is truth?"

After he had said this, he went back outside to the Jews and told them, "I find no guilt in him. [39][a]But you have a custom that I should release one man for you at the Passover. So do you want me to release to you the King of the Jews?" [40]They cried out again, "Not this man, but Barabbas!" Now Barabbas was a robber.[1]

DAY 25

Jesus Delivered to Be Crucified

19Then Pilate took Jesus and flogged him. [2]And the soldiers twisted together a crown of thorns and put it on his head and arrayed him in a purple robe. [3]They came up to him, saying, "Hail, King of the Jews!" and struck him with their hands. [4]Pilate went out again and said to them, "See, I am bringing him out to you that you may know that I find no guilt in him." [5]So Jesus came out, wearing the crown of thorns and the purple robe. Pilate said to them, "Behold the man!" [6]When the chief priests and the officers saw him, they cried out, "Crucify him, crucify him!" Pilate said to them, "Take him yourselves and crucify him, for I find no guilt in him." [7]The Jews[2] answered him, "We have a law, and according to that law he ought to die because he has made himself the Son of God." [8]When Pilate heard this statement, he was even more afraid. [9]He entered his headquarters again and said to Jesus, "Where are you from?" But Jesus gave him no answer. [10]So Pilate said to him, "You will not speak to me? Do you not know that I have authority to release you and authority to crucify you?" [11]Jesus answered him, "You would have no authority over me at all unless it had been given you from above. Therefore he who delivered me over to you has the greater sin."

[12]From then on Pilate sought to release him, but the Jews cried out, "If you release this man, you are not Caesar's friend. Everyone who makes himself a king opposes Caesar." [13]So when Pilate heard these words, he brought Jesus out and sat down on the judgment seat at a place called The Stone Pavement, and in Aramaic[3] Gabbatha. [14]Now it was the day of Preparation of the Passover. It was about the sixth hour.[4] He said to the Jews, "Behold your King!" [15]They cried out, "Away with him, away with

[1]Or an insurrectionist [2]Greek Ioudaioi probably refers here to Jewish religious leaders, and others under their influence, in that time; also verses 12, 14, 31, 38 [3]Or Hebrew; also verses 17, 20 [4]That is, about noon [a]For 18:39, 40 see parallels Matt. 27:15-18, 20-23; Mark 15:6-14; Luke 23:18-23

him, crucify him!" Pilate said to them, "Shall I crucify your King?" The chief priests answered, "We have no king but Caesar."

DAY 26

[16]So he delivered him over to them to be crucified.

The Crucifixion

So they took Jesus, [17]and he went out, bearing his own cross, to the place called The Place of a Skull, which in Aramaic is called Golgotha. [18]There they crucified him, and with him two others, one on either side, and Jesus between them. [19]Pilate also wrote an inscription and put it on the cross. It read, "Jesus of Nazareth, the King of the Jews." [20]Many of the Jews read this inscription, for the place where Jesus was crucified was near the city, and it was written in Aramaic, in Latin, and in Greek. [21]So the chief priests of the Jews said to Pilate, "Do not write, 'The King of the Jews,' but rather, 'This man said, I am King of the Jews.'" [22]Pilate answered, "What I have written I have written."

[23]When the soldiers had crucified Jesus, they took his garments and divided them into four parts, one part for each soldier; also his tunic.[1] But the tunic was seamless, woven in one piece from top to bottom, [24]so they said to one another, "Let us not tear it, but cast lots for it to see whose it shall be." This was to fulfill the Scripture which says,

[a]"They divided my garments among them,
    and for my clothing they cast lots."

So the soldiers did these things, [25]but standing by the cross of Jesus were his mother and his mother's sister, Mary the wife of Clopas, and Mary Magdalene. [26]When Jesus saw his mother and the disciple whom he loved standing nearby, he said to his mother, "Woman, behold, your son!" [27]Then he said to the disciple, "Behold, your mother!" And from that hour the disciple took her to his own home.

The Death of Jesus

[28]After this, Jesus, knowing that all was now finished, said (to fulfill the Scripture), "I thirst." [29]A jar full of sour wine stood there, so they put a sponge full of the sour wine on a hyssop branch and held it to his mouth. [30]When Jesus had received the sour wine, he said, "It is finished," and he bowed his head and gave up his spirit.

[1]Greek *chiton*, a long garment worn under the cloak next to the skin [a]Ps. 22:18

DAY 27

Jesus' Side Is Pierced

³¹Since it was the day of Preparation, and so that the bodies would not remain on the cross on the Sabbath (for that Sabbath was a high day), the Jews asked Pilate that their legs might be broken and that they might be taken away. ³²So the soldiers came and broke the legs of the first, and of the other who had been crucified with him. ³³But when they came to Jesus and saw that he was already dead, they did not break his legs. ³⁴But one of the soldiers pierced his side with a spear, and at once there came out blood and water. ³⁵He who saw it has borne witness—his testimony is true, and he knows that he is telling the truth—that you also may believe. ³⁶For these things took place that the Scripture might be fulfilled: ᵃ"Not one of his bones will be broken." ³⁷And again another Scripture says, ᵇ"They will look on him whom they have pierced."

Jesus Is Buried

³⁸ᶜAfter these things Joseph of Arimathea, who was a disciple of Jesus, but secretly for fear of the Jews, asked Pilate that he might take away the body of Jesus, and Pilate gave him permission. So he came and took away his body. ³⁹Nicodemus also, who earlier had come to Jesus¹ by night, came bringing a mixture of myrrh and aloes, about seventy-five pounds² in weight. ⁴⁰So they took the body of Jesus and bound it in linen cloths with the spices, as is the burial custom of the Jews. ⁴¹Now in the place where he was crucified there was a garden, and in the garden a new tomb in which no one had yet been laid. ⁴²So because of the Jewish day of Preparation, since the tomb was close at hand, they laid Jesus there.

DAY 28

The Resurrection

20 Now on the first day of the week Mary Magdalene came to the tomb early, while it was still dark, and saw that the stone had been taken away from the tomb. ²So she ran and went to Simon Peter and the other disciple, the one whom Jesus loved, and said to them, "They have taken the Lord out of the tomb, and we do not know where they have laid him." ³So Peter went out with the other disciple, and they were going toward the tomb. ⁴Both of them were running together, but the other

¹Greek *him* ²Greek *one hundred litras*; a *litra* (or Roman pound) was equal to about 11 1/2 ounces or 327 grams ᵃEx. 12:46; Num. 9:12 ᵇZech. 12:10 ᶜFor 19:38-42 see parallels Matt. 27:57-61; Mark 15:42-47; Luke 23:50-56

disciple outran Peter and reached the tomb first. [5]And stooping to look in, he saw the linen cloths lying there, but he did not go in. [6]Then Simon Peter came, following him, and went into the tomb. He saw the linen cloths lying there, [7]and the face cloth, which had been on Jesus'[1] head, not lying with the linen cloths but folded up in a place by itself. [8]Then the other disciple, who had reached the tomb first, also went in, and he saw and believed; [9]for as yet they did not understand the Scripture, that he must rise from the dead. [10]Then the disciples went back to their homes.

Jesus Appears to Mary Magdalene

[11]But Mary stood weeping outside the tomb, and as she wept she stooped to look into the tomb. [12]And she saw two angels in white, sitting where the body of Jesus had lain, one at the head and one at the feet. [13]They said to her, "Woman, why are you weeping?" She said to them, "They have taken away my Lord, and I do not know where they have laid him." [14]Having said this, she turned around and saw Jesus standing, but she did not know that it was Jesus. [15]Jesus said to her, "Woman, why are you weeping? Whom are you seeking?" Supposing him to be the gardener, she said to him, "Sir, if you have carried him away, tell me where you have laid him, and I will take him away." [16]Jesus said to her, "Mary." She turned and said to him in Aramaic,[2] "Rabboni!" (which means Teacher). [17]Jesus said to her, "Do not cling to me, for I have not yet ascended to the Father; but go to my brothers and say to them, 'I am ascending to my Father and your Father, to my God and your God.'" [18]Mary Magdalene went and announced to the disciples, "I have seen the Lord"—and that he had said these things to her.

DAY 29

Jesus Appears to the Disciples

[19]On the evening of that day, the first day of the week, the doors being locked where the disciples were for fear of the Jews,[3] Jesus came and stood among them and said to them, "Peace be with you." [20]When he had said this, he showed them his hands and his side. Then the disciples were glad when they saw the Lord. [21]Jesus said to them again, "Peace be with you. As the Father has sent me, even so I am sending you." [22]And when he had said this, he breathed on them and said to them, "Receive the Holy Spirit. [23]If you forgive the sins of any, they are forgiven them; if you withhold forgiveness from any, it is withheld."

[1]Greek *his* [2]Or *Hebrew* [3]Greek *Ioudaioi* probably refers here to Jewish religious leaders, and others under their influence, in that time

Jesus and Thomas

²⁴Now Thomas, one of the twelve, called the Twin,ᶦ was not with them when Jesus came. ²⁵So the other disciples told him, "We have seen the Lord." But he said to them, "Unless I see in his hands the mark of the nails, and place my finger into the mark of the nails, and place my hand into his side, I will never believe."

²⁶Eight days later, his disciples were inside again, and Thomas was with them. Although the doors were locked, Jesus came and stood among them and said, "Peace be with you." ²⁷Then he said to Thomas, "Put your finger here, and see my hands; and put out your hand, and place it in my side. Do not disbelieve, but believe." ²⁸Thomas answered him, "My Lord and my God!" ²⁹Jesus said to him, "Have you believed because you have seen me? Blessed are those who have not seen and yet have believed."

The Purpose of This Book

³⁰Now Jesus did many other signs in the presence of the disciples, which are not written in this book; ³¹but these are written so that you may believe that Jesus is the Christ, the Son of God, and that by believing you may have life in his name.

DAY 30

Jesus Appears to Seven Disciples

21After this Jesus revealed himself again to the disciples by the Sea of Tiberias, and he revealed himself in this way. ²Simon Peter, Thomas (called the Twin), Nathanael of Cana in Galilee, the sons of Zebedee, and two others of his disciples were together. ³Simon Peter said to them, "I am going fishing." They said to him, "We will go with you." They went out and got into the boat, but that night they caught nothing.

⁴Just as day was breaking, Jesus stood on the shore; yet the disciples did not know that it was Jesus. ⁵Jesus said to them, "Children, do you have any fish?" They answered him, "No." ⁶He said to them, "Cast the net on the right side of the boat, and you will find some." So they cast it, and now they were not able to haul it in, because of the quantity of fish. ⁷That disciple whom Jesus loved therefore said to Peter, "It is the Lord!" When Simon Peter heard that it was the Lord, he put on his outer garment, for he was stripped for work, and threw himself into the sea. ⁸The other disciples came in the boat, dragging the net full of fish, for they were not far from the land, but about a hundred yards² off.

ᶦGreek *Didymus* ²Greek *two hundred cubits*; a cubit was about 18 inches or 45 centimeters

92

⁹When they got out on land, they saw a charcoal fire in place, with fish laid out on it, and bread. ¹⁰Jesus said to them, "Bring some of the fish that you have just caught." ¹¹So Simon Peter went aboard and hauled the net ashore, full of large fish, 153 of them. And although there were so many, the net was not torn. ¹²Jesus said to them, "Come and have breakfast." Now none of the disciples dared ask him, "Who are you?" They knew it was the Lord. ¹³Jesus came and took the bread and gave it to them, and so with the fish. ¹⁴This was now the third time that Jesus was revealed to the disciples after he was raised from the dead.

Jesus and Peter

¹⁵When they had finished breakfast, Jesus said to Simon Peter, "Simon, son of John, do you love me more than these?" He said to him, "Yes, Lord; you know that I love you." He said to him, "Feed my lambs." ¹⁶He said to him a second time, "Simon, son of John, do you love me?" He said to him, "Yes, Lord; you know that I love you." He said to him, "Tend my sheep." ¹⁷He said to him the third time, "Simon, son of John, do you love me?" Peter was grieved because he said to him the third time, "Do you love me?" and he said to him, "Lord, you know everything; you know that I love you." Jesus said to him, "Feed my sheep. ¹⁸Truly, truly, I say to you, when you were young, you used to dress yourself and walk wherever you wanted, but when you are old, you will stretch out your hands, and another will dress you and carry you where you do not want to go." ¹⁹(This he said to show by what kind of death he was to glorify God.) And after saying this he said to him, "Follow me."

Jesus and the Beloved Apostle

²⁰Peter turned and saw the disciple whom Jesus loved following them, the one who also had leaned back against him during the supper and had said, "Lord, who is it that is going to betray you?" ²¹When Peter saw him, he said to Jesus, "Lord, what about this man?" ²²Jesus said to him, "If it is my will that he remain until I come, what is that to you? You follow me!" ²³So the saying spread abroad among the brothers¹ that this disciple was not to die; yet Jesus did not say to him that he was not to die, but, "If it is my will that he remain until I come, what is that to you?"

²⁴This is the disciple who is bearing witness about these things, and who has written these things, and we know that his testimony is true.

²⁵Now there are also many other things that Jesus did. Were every one of them to be written, I suppose that the world itself could not contain the books that would be written.

¹Or brothers and sisters

NOTES

NOTES

NOTES